Passport to German

CHARLES BERLITZ

Travel Information Supplied
by David Butwin

A SIGNET BOOK
NEW AMERICAN LIBRARY
TIMES MIRROR

SIGNET TRADEMARK REG. U.S. PAT. OFF. AND FOREIGN COUNTRIES
REGISTERED TRADEMARK—MARCA REGISTRADA
HECHO EN CHICAGO, U.S.A.

SIGNET, SIGNET CLASSICS, MENTOR, PLUME, MERIDIAN AND NAL
BOOKS are published by The New American Library, Inc.,
1633 Broadway, New York, New York 10019

First Signet Printing, April, 1974

7 8 9 10 11 12 13 14

PRINTED IN THE UNITED STATES OF AMERICA

 Contents

One of the misconceptions about modern Germany that diverts travelers to other lands is that the country is too modernized and industrialized to offer any old-fashioned beauty. The truth is that if you keep away from the booming smokestack forests of the Ruhr and other areas, you will find a peaceful, fairy-tale land, such as the Romantic Road, which meanders south from Würzburg through such splendidly unspoiled towns as Dinkelsbühl and Rothenburg. An altogether different experience is a visit to Berlin, hardly a shadow of its once proud and artistic self but nonetheless a compelling place, and one that still manages to stay loud and awake every night until dawn. Nor are German prices as high as people fear, at least not in the outlying regions away from such commercial centers as Hamburg, Frankfurt, and Munich.

Where to Stay

Accommodations are so varied in Germany that you can even spend the night in a barrel. At Rüdesheim on the Rhine, the proprietor of the Hotel Lindenwirt has converted six wine casks, each with a capacity of 1,600 gallons, into double bedrooms with built-in closets and private baths. Bed and breakfast amount to less than $7 per person. Or you can spend a week on a farm in the Black Forest, with some meals included, for less than $50. It's less if you want to pitch in with the milking and haying. Hotel packages have been created to attract various types of people—one hotel even throws in sky-diving lessons.

More traditional lodging can be arranged in any *Verkehrsverein*, or tourist bureau, near local train stations. Pensions, or *Gasthauser*, with simple appointments and prices ($3 to $4) are spread throughout the country, and an even cheaper proposition is a *stuben*, or tavern, with a sign out front advertising guest rooms, *Fremden Zimmer*. Private homes often let rooms for under $3. Holiday Inn is entrenching itself in Germany, with seventeen open, under construction, or planned by late 1971. Prices are reasonable if you can put up with American-style *Gemütlichkeit*.

Germany has more castle-hotels than any other country, and most offer low rates in the off-season. Among the fifty or so are medieval fortresses and eighteenth- and nineteenth-century manor houses. Kronberg near Frankfurt is a stunning example of a manor house—chock-full of velvet carpets, tapestries, chandeliers, thick beams, and busts of former tenants. Less than a century old, it was built in 1888 for Queen Victoria's eldest daughter, the mother of Emperor Wilhelm II.

Other castles with rooms for rent: Burg Lauenstein in Bayreuth, a thousand years old, is walled in by a ring of guardhouses and deep fir woods. One night with breakfast costs only about $4.50. Lauenstein has thirty-five beds; many of the other castles have twenty or twenty-five. Hotel Schloss Weitenburg in the Neckar Valley was first built in the twelfth century, destroyed by fire, and rebuilt to its present shape in the 1700s. Today's owner, Baron von Rassler, will take guests out to ride and shoot game. South of Hanover, in Grimm fairy-tale country, lies the century-old estate Trendelburg. Baron von Stockhausen and his wife are gastronomes and prepare such feasts as trout à la poacher served on hot bricks. The Schonburg at Oberwesel, a medieval castle, looms high above a wine-growing town on the left bank of the Rhine. Its culinary specialty is frogs' legs cooked in Riesling wine.

How to Eat

In restaurants, a fixed-price menu offers the best bargain: soup, main dish, vegetable, potato or dumpling, and dessert for a few dollars. Another mark or two brings a stein of beer or local table wine such as a Moselle or Rhine wine.

Among Germany's inexpensive and filling restaurants are the 300 Wienerwalds, which specialize in spit-roasted chicken (one-half chicken for $1.50) and chicken soup. Against a faintly Viennese backdrop you can also order *kassler rippchen* (smoked loin of pork with sauerkraut), assorted schnitzel, other German specialties, or even a good Magyar goulash. Munich has 29 branches; Hamburg, 7; Cologne, 6; Manhattan, 4. At any Chico shop, a traveler willing to drink his coffee standing up can do so for 8 cents. Big department stores such as Neckermann, Herties, Kauhof, and Karstadt serve a full lunch for under $1. *Bierstube* and *Weinstube* (beer and wine establishments) sometimes offer a wurst or other snack, and you can often carry your mug out back into a garden. *Schnell Imbiss* and *Wursterei* sell good, ample lunches, assembled in minutes. There is a fifteen percent surcharge if you want to sit down. At Die Fisch Mutter in West Berlin, the mother herself has been feeding hungry students since 1925. A huge slab of fish plus all the potato salad you can eat costs under $1.

There is always that German institution known as *leberkäse*. Translated, it means liver-cheese, but actually it has no cheese and only a little liver. It's mostly meat, and every butcher shop in southern Germany, especially in Munich, has it. The sign in the window will say *Warmer Leberkäse*. You can also buy loops of wursts, which hang in windows of butcher shops or are sold by street vendors. In late spring, every restaurant in the Palatinate region serves a German favorite called *spargel*—tender white asparagus that can be prepared dozens of ways and, with meat and cream sauce, can be almost a meal in itself.

What to Buy

Among the traditionally fine German products to buy are optical objects such as binoculars, microscopes, magnifying glasses, and especially cameras, such as Rolleiflex and Leica. Other specialties are cutlery, crystal and blown glass, luggage and leather goods, *lederhosen* and dirndl skirts. Lately *lederhosen*, made from skins that have been cured for thirteen months, have been slightly altered and turned into hot pants. Prices on most products run about a third lower than they would be in the United States.

Another popular, if unusual, buy is a personal plaster, bronze, or silver mask from Helga Borgk, Maienstrasse 4, 1 Berlin 30. The procedure takes fifteen minutes, the plaster drying in two minutes. Helga will turn you out in miniature for $27 or $21. Busts of the same material cost $250-$375. Delivery of the masks takes three days.

The German fashion centers are Munich, Berlin, and Düsseldorf. Small dressmakers and in some cases leading couturiers will run up an ensemble in as little as three days. One of Germany's best-known designers is Werner Machnik, whose daytime dresses cost from $85-$400 and whose evening gowns start at $250. But surprising off-the-rack bargains can be found in any department store.

How to Travel

Geographically narrowed by the war, Germany rebuilt its rail system on a north-south axis, and by the Munich Olympics of 1972, an intercity network will link up seventy-two cities with high-speed service, and three prototype electric self-propelled trains will breeze at 125 mph between Bremen and Munich. West Berlin's Bahnhofzoo, a buzzing Grand Central before the war, has been reduced, however, to an all but vacant barn, with only several trains a day pulling out for the west.

West German railroads have launched a system permitting Eurailpass holders to have their baggage picked up at one hotel and delivered to the next so they don't have to lug it aboard. The charge is 50 cents for 110 pounds. Americans are sometimes surprised at the do-it-yourself style practiced in most European depots. Germany, though, has introduced self-service shopping carts and baggage-check compartments in major terminals.

To cross the border by rail en route to West Berlin you need a valid passport and a transit visa issued on the train for $2.50 round trip. But since air fares to West Berlin are subsidized, it's almost as cheap and much more convenient to fly into Templehof Airport. A rail–air comparison shows that a one-way first-class ticket by train from Frankfurt to Berlin is $21.20 plus transit visa—by plane, $24.20 and no visa. The cheapest city to fly from is Hanover.

Hitchhiking is not particularly recommended for Germany and is in fact illegal on the autobahns. Driving these superhighways takes a certain adjustment. For one thing, there is no speed limit. Signal well ahead when passing a car, check your rearview mirror, then make the pass and return to the right lane. When a German driver wants you to pull over and let him pass, he'll blink his light several times. Drivers are not permitted to leave the autobahn and may stop only for emergencies.

What to Do

Travelers and tourist promoters agree that Rhine cruises get to the heart of German life. The great white ships leave from Cologne or Bonn and sail past castles high above vine-covered hills. The KD–German Rhine Line offers cruises from a few hours to five days in length; one common run, upstream from Koblenz to Mainz, a seven-hour trip, costs a little more than $4. Along the way one or two marks (under $1) will buy a castle tour and passengers can take lunch in a castle café or riverside restaurant. Every mile of the trip tells something about German history.

If a Rhine cruise seems *too* traditional, there is always the Weser, winding through some of the least tainted of German countryside, passing ancient towns like Hoxter with its sixteenth- and seventeenth-century half-timbered houses. Steamer trips along the Upper Weser begin in midspring, connecting Hameln with Hannoversch Münden.

Steamer tours run four, five, seven, or eleven days.

Another popular venture would be into a German beer hall. The country's largest, and probably its most boisterous, is Munich's Hofbräuhaus at Platzl 9. The mugs that have become its symbol—heavy, blue-gray, and embossed with a crown and the initials "HB"—decorate rooms around the world. A full liter of beer costs only about 50 cents.

Perhaps the liveliest time to arrive in Germany—and also one of the cheapest—is late September through mid-October when the annual Oktoberfest explodes in Munich. Everyone, including the mayor, who taps the first barrel, crowds into Theresie Meadow to consume a half million gallons of beer. In late winter, carnival parades wind through Cologne, Düsseldorf, and Mainz, while Munich celebrates the *Fasching*. The Bremen Free Market opens in October and the Dom Festival in Hamburg in late fall. In the Harz, residents celebrate "Walpurgis night"; in Durkheim, the "sausage market"; in Schwabisch Hall, "the salt boilers festival." Hameln honors the Pied Piper, who lured rats and children out of the town in the Middle Ages.

You don't even need a schedule to find a German festival. A frequent visitor to Germany suggests: "At noon on Friday, board a train in Hamburg and head north for the provinces. Twenty or thirty kilometers north and you're in Schleswig Holstein. If you notice a lot of banners at smaller stations, you've probably hit a riding festival, rifle festival, or fire department festival. In the afternoon, there might be contests like target shooting or tests of strength. In the evening—beer tents, music, carousels, sausage stands, and dancing. You'll meet the mayor, the teacher, the rifle champ, the police chief. It might happen that around midnight, they'll make you an honorary citizen of Rellingen, of Klingsbuhl, or Moorneudorf."

—DAVID BUTWIN

NOTE: *Prices in dollars will vary according to whatever rate of exchange is in effect at a given time.*

🌻 How to Acquire an Instant German Accent

Every word or sentence in this book is presented in English, in German, and in an easy-to-read phonetic system that shows you how to pronounce the German correctly. Just pronounce the phonetics as if you were reading English, remembering the following special points:

Syllables printed in capital letters should be stressed.

The syllables are separated by hyphens, except the verb ending -en, which is to be pronounced almost as a part of the preceding syllable and for that reason is separated just by an apostrophe. (The apostrophe is also sometimes used between sounds within a syllable to help you see more easily how to pronounce them.)

To pronounce the sound of the special symbol *ü* used in the phonetics, say "ee" but with your lips rounded in a tight little circle as if to whistle. The small circle is to remind you to round your lips.

When you see the combination of letters *kh* in the phonetics, pronounce it with a guttural, throaty sound—like a rough "h" deep in the throat.

When *er* is used in the phonetics and the spelling in the German word is ö, pronounce it as in the English word "fern" but make the "r" as silent as possible. (Of course, when the letter r appears in the German spelling, then you should pronounce it fully.)

The letter *g* is always pronounced as in "go" or "get," never as in "gem." To help you remember this, we have spelled it *gh* in the phonetics when it comes before an *e* or an *i*.

The combination *ow* in the phonetics is always pronounced as in "how now, brown cow." We have put an apostrophe before it in such syllables as *l'ow* and *t'ow* to remind you not to pronounce them like the English words "low" and "tow."

The German pronunciation is made clear in the phonetic lines in this book, but it will be helpful for you in reading any other written German you may encounter if you also remember the following differences between German and English spelling and pronunciation:

b when it comes at the end of a word is pronounced *p*.

d when it comes at the end of a word is pronounced *t*.

g when it comes at the end of a word is pronounced *k* (or with the guttural *kh* sound in the combination **-ig**).

j is pronounced like the English *y*.

qu is pronounced *kv*.

v is pronounced like English *f*.

w is pronounced like English *v*.

s when it comes at the beginning of a word and usually in the middle of a word is pronounced like English *z*. At the end of a word it is always pronounced *ss*.

sp and **st** at the beginning of a word are pronounced *shp* and *sht* respectively.

The special German letter **ß** (called *"ess-ts'et"*) is pronounced *ss*.

z is pronounced *ts*.

ch is the guttural *kh* sound.

sch is pronounced like English *sh*.

The vowels **a, e, i, o,** and **u** are pronounced *ah, eh, ee* (or *ih*), *oh,* and *oo* respectively.

ei is pronounced like the English word "eye," and **ie** is pronounced *ee;* **eu** is pronounced *oy*.

When the vowels are written in German with two dots over them, they are called "umlauts," and their approximate pronunciations are as follows: **ä,** *eh;* **äu,** *oy;* **ö,** like *er* but with the sound of the "r" silent; and **ü,** like *ee* with the lips tightly rounded.

If you follow the advice we have given you and the simple phonetics under each word in the book, you are certain to be told:

Sie haben eine sehr gute Aussprache!

zee HAHB'en INE-eh zair GOOT-eh OWSS-shpra-kheh! which means, "You have a very good accent!"

🦅 1. Greetings and Introductions

Mr.	Sir	Mrs.
Herr	Mein Herr	Frau
hair	*mine hair*	*frow*

Madame	Miss
Gnädige Frau	Fräulein
G'NAY-dee-ghe frow	*FROY-line*

Good morning!	Good day.	Good evening.
Guten Morgen!	Guten Tag.	Guten Abend.
GOO-ten MOR-ghen!	*GOO-ten tahk.*	*GOO-ten AH-bent.*

How are you?	Fine, thanks, and you?
Wie geht es Ihnen?	Gut, danke, und Ihnen?
vee gait ess EEN-en?	*goot, DAHN-keh, oont EEN-en?*

Come in, please.	Sit down, please!
Kommen Sie herein, bitte.	Nehmen Sie Platz, bitte!
KOHM'en zee hair-INE, BIT-teh.	*NAIM'en zee plahts, BIT-teh.*

My name is Krüger.	What is your name?
Mein Name ist Krüger.	Wie ist Ihr Name?
mine NA-meh isst KRÜ-gher.	*vee isst eer NA-meh?*

May I introduce ———.	Delighted (to meet you).
Darf ich vorstellen ———.	Sehr angenehm.
darf ikh FOR-shtel'en ———.	*zair AHN-ghe-naim.*

---

1. Pronounce *ü* like "ee" with your lips in a tight circle.
2. *kh* is a guttural sound.
3. Stress the syllables in capital letters.

Good-bye.	So long.	Good night.
Auf Wiedersehen.	Bis bald.	Gute Nacht.
owf VEE-der-zain.	*biss bahlt.*	*GOOT-eh nakht.*

In southern Germany, Austria, and Switzerland a general greeting for all occasions is **Grüss' Gott**—the equivalent of "God bless you."

🦅 2. Basic Expressions

Learn these by heart. You will use them every time you speak German to someone. If you memorize these expressions and the numbers in the next section you will find that you can ask prices or directions and generally make your wishes known.

Yes.	No.	Perhaps.
Ja.	Nein.	Vielleicht.
ya.	*nine.*	*feel-LY'KHT.*

Of course.	Yes indeed.	Please.
Natürlich.	Jawohl.	Bitte.
na-TÜR-likh.	*ya-VOHL.*	*BIT-teh.*

Thank you.	You are welcome.
Danke schön.	Bitte sehr.
DAHN-keh shern.	*BIT-teh zair.*

Excuse me.	I'm sorry.	It's all right.
Entschuldigung.	Es tut mir leid.	Es macht nichts.
ent-SHOOL-dee-goong.	*ess toot meer lite.*	*ess makht nikhts.*

Here.	There.	This.	That.
Hier.	Dort.	Dies.	Das.
heer.	*dort.*	*deess.*	*dahss.*

Do you speak English?	I speak a little German.
Sprechen Sie Englisch?	Ich spreche ein wenig Deutsch.
SHPREKH'en zee EHNG-lish?	*ikh SHPREKH-eh ine VAY-nikh doytch.*

---

1. Pronounce *ü* like "ee" with your lips in a tight circle.
2. *kh* is a guttural sound.
3. Stress the syllables in capital letters.

Do you understand?
Verstehen Sie?
fair-SHTAY'en zee?

I understand.
Ich verstehe.
ikh fair-SHTAY-eh.

. . . very well.
. . . sehr gut.
. . . *zair goot.*

I don't understand.
Ich verstehe nicht.
ikh fair-SHTAY-eh nikht.

Speak slowly, please.
Sprechen Sie langsam, bitte.
SHPREKH'en zee
LAHNG-zahm, BIT-teh.

Repeat, please.
Wiederholen Sie, bitte.
vee-der-HO-len zee, BIT-
teh.

Write it down.
Schreiben Sie es auf.
SHRY-ben zee ess owf.

Who is it?
Wer ist es?
vair isst ess?

Come in!
Herein!
hair-INE!

Don't come in!
Kommen Sie nicht herein!
KOHM'en zee nikht hair-INE!

One moment, please.
Einen Moment, bitte.
INE-en mo-MENT, BIT-teh.

Wait.
Warten Sie.
VAR-ten zee.

Let's go!
Gehen wir.
GAY'en veer.

That's all.
Das ist alles.
dahss isst AHL-less.

What is this?
Was ist das?
vahss isst dahss?

Where is is the telephone?
Wo ist das Telefon?
vo isst dahss teh-leh-FOHN?

Where is the restroom?
Wo ist die Toilette?
vo isst dee twa-LET-teh?

For ladies.
Für Damen.
für DA-men.

For men.
Für Herren.
fur HAIR-ren.

Show me.
Zeigen Sie mir.
TS'EYE-ghen zee meer.

How much?
Wieviel?
vee-FEEL?

It's too much.	**Who?**
Das ist zu viel.	Wer?
dahss isst ts'oo feel.	*vair?*

I	**you**	**he**	**she**
Ich	Sie	er	sie
ikh	*zee*	*air*	*zee*

it	**we**	**they**
es	wir	sie
ess	*veer*	*zee*

How far is it?	**How long?**
Wie weit ist es?	Wie lange?
vee vite isst ess?	*vee LAHNG-eh?*

How?	**Like this.**	**Not like this.**
Wie?	So.	Nicht so.
vee?	*zo.*	*nikht zo.*

It is possible.	**It is not possible.**
Es ist möglich.	Es ist nicht möglich.
ess isst MERG-likh.	*ess isst nikht MERG-likh.*

When?	**Now.**	**Not now.**
Wann?	Jetzt.	Nicht jetzt.
vahn?	*yetst.*	*nikht yetst.*

Later.	**That is very good.**
Später.	Das ist sehr gut.
SHPAY-ter.	*dahss isst zair goot.*

That is bad.	**Really?**
Das ist schlecht.	Wirklich?
dahss isst shlekht.	*VEERK-likh?*

---

1. Pronounce *ü* like "ee" with your lips in a tight circle.
2. *kh* is a guttural sound.
3. Stress the syllables in capital letters.

It doesn't matter.
Es macht nichts.
ess mahkht nikhts.

It's very important.
Est ist sehr wichtig.
ess isst zehr VIKH-tikh.

You should always use **bitte**, which means "please" (and also "You are welcome"), when you ask questions or make requests. It can also function for "Bring me . . .," "I want . . .," or "I would like . . .," etc. Simply say **bitte** followed by the word for whatever you want, which you can find in the dictionary section.

Nicht wahr? as a question can be used to request agreement to something or to mean "Isn't it?" "Isn't that right?" or "Don't you think so?"

🦅 3. Numbers

The numbers are important not only for asking prices (and perhaps to bargain) but for phone numbers, addresses, and telling time. Learn the first twenty by heart and then from 20 to 100 by tens and you can deal with money (Geld), a telephone number (eine Telefonnummer), or an address (eine Adresse).

1	**2**	**3**	**4**
eins	zwei	drei	vier
ine'ss	*ts'vy*	*dry*	*feer*

5	**6**	**7**	**8**
fünf	sechs	sieben	acht
fünf	*zeks*	*ZEE-ben*	*ahkht*

9	**10**	**11**	**12**
neun	zehn	elf	zwölf
noyn	*ts'ayn*	*elf*	*ts'verlf*

13	**14**	**15**
dreizehn	vierzehn	fünfzehn
DRY-ts'ayn	*FEER-ts'ayn*	*FÜNF-ts'ayn*

16	**17**	**18**
sechzehn	siebzehn	achtzehn
ZEKH-ts'ayn	*ZEEP-ts'ayn*	*AHKH-ts'ayn*

19	**20**	**21**
neunzehn	zwanzig	einundzwanzig
NOYN-ts'ayn	*TS'VAHN-ts'ikh*	*INE-oont-ts'vahn-ts'ikh*

---

1. Pronounce *ü* like "ee" with your lips in a tight circle.
2. *kh* is a guttural sound.
3. Stress the syllables in capital letters.

22
zweiundzwanzig
TS'VY-oont-ts'vahn-ts'ikh

23
dreiundzwanzig
DRY-oont-ts'vahn-ts'ikh

24
vierundzwanzig
FEER-oont-ts'vahn-ts'ikh

25
fünfundzwanzig
FÜNF-oont-ts'vahn-ts'ikh

30
dreißig
DRY-sikh

40
vierzig
FEER-ts'ikh

50
fünfzig
FÜNF-ts'ikh

60
sechzig
ZEKH-ts'ikh

70
siebzig
ZEEP-ts'ikh

80
achtzig
AHKH-ts'ikh

90
neunzig
NOYN-ts'ikh

100
(ein) hundert
(ine) HOON-dert

200
zweihundert
TS'VY-hoon-dert

300
dreihundert
DRY-hoon-dert

400
vierhundert
FEER-hoon-dert

500
fünfhundert
FÜNF-hoon-dert

600
sechshundert
ZEKS-hoon-dert

700
siebenhundert
ZEE-ben-hoon-dert

800
achthundert
AHKHT-hoon-dert

900
neunhundert
NOYN-hoon-dert

1000
eintausend
ine-T'OW-zent

2000
zweitausend
TS'VY-t'ow-zent

3000
dreitausend
DRY-t'ow-zent

100,000
hunderttausend
HOON-dert-t'ow-zent

1,000,000
eine Million
INE-eh MIL-yohn

the first	the second	the third
der erste	der zweite	der dritte
dair AIR-steh	*dair TS'VY-teh*	*dair DRIT-eh*

the last	half	zero
der letzte	halb	null
dair LETS-teh	*hahlp*	*nool*

How much? (or) How many?   **What number?**
Wieviel?   Welche Nummer?
vee-FEEL?   *VEL-kheh NOOM-er?*

The number 2, **zwei**, is often called **zwo** (*tsvo*) because, especially over the telephone, **zwei** sounds like **drei**.

"The" is **der** for a masculine noun, **die** for a feminine noun, **das** for a neuter noun, all in the singular. For the plural, "the" becomes **die** for all three genders.

# 4. Arrival

Besides talking with airport officials, one of the most important things you will want to do on arrival in Germany, Austria, or Switzerland is to find your way about. In this section you will find some basic "asking your way" questions and answers. We call your attention to the "Point to the Answer" sections, which people can use to *point out* answers to make it easier for you to understand.

Your passport, please.	**I am here on a visit.**
Ihren Pass, bitte.	Ich bin hier auf Besuch.
EER-en pahss BIT-teh.	*ikh bin heer owf beh-ZOOKH.*
For three weeks.	**I am on a business trip.**
Für drei Wochen.	Ich bin auf Geschäftsreise.
für dry VO-khen.	*ikh bin owf ghe-SHEHFTS-rye-zeh.*
Where is the customs office?	**Where is your baggage?**
Wo ist das Zollamt?	Wo ist Ihr Gepäck?
vo isst dahss TS'OL-ahmt?	*vo isst eer ghe-PAYK?*
My bags are over there.	**Those there.**
Mein Gepäck ist dort.	Das dort.
mine ghe-PAYK isst dort.	*dahss dort.*
That belongs to me.	**Shall I open it?**
Das gehört mir.	Soll ich es aufmachen?
dahss ghe-HERT meer.	*zoll ikh ess OWF-mahkh'en?*
Open it.	**One moment, please.**
Machen Sie es auf.	Einen Moment, bitte.
MAHKH'en zee ess owf.	*INE-en mo-MENT, BIT-teh.*

I am looking for the key.
Ich suche den Schlüssel.
ikh ZOO-kheh den SHLÜSS-el.

I have nothing to declare.
Ich habe nichts zu verzollen.
ikh HAHB-eh nikhts ts'oo fair-TS'OLL'en.

This is for my private use.
Dies ist für meinen Privatgebrauch.
deess isst für MY-nen pree-VAHT-ghe-browkh.

These are gifts.
Das sind Geschenke.
dahss zint ghe-SHENK-eh.

Must I pay something?
Habe ich etwas zu bezahlen?
HAHB-eh ikh ET-vahss ts'oo beh-TS'AHL'en?

Where is the bus to the city?
Wo ist der Bus zur Stadt?
vo isst dair booss ts'oor shtaht?

Where can I make a phone call?
Wo kann ich telefonieren?
vo kahn ikh teh-leh-foh-NEER'en?

Where is the restaurant?
Wo ist das Restaurant?
vo isst dahss rest-oh-RAHNG?

Where are the restrooms?
Wo sind die Toiletten?
vo zint dee twah-LET-en?

Porter!
Gepäckträger!
ghe-PAYK-tray-gher!

Take these bags to a taxi.
Bringen Sie diese Koffer zu
einem Taxi.
*BRING'en zee DEE-zeh
KOFF-er ts'oo INE-em
TAHK-see.*

---

1. Pronounce ü like "ee" with your lips in a tight circle.
2. *kh* is a guttural sound.
3. Stress the syllables in capital letters.

I'll carry this one myself.
Ich trage diesen selbst.
ikh TRAHG-eh DEE-zen zelpst.

How much is it?
Wieviel macht es?
vee-FEEL mahkt ess?

To the Hotel Frankfurter Hof.
Zum Hotel Frankfurter Hof.
ts'oom ho-TEL frahnk-foor-ter hohf.

To the Hotel Vier Jahreszeiten, please.
Zum Hotel Vier Jahreszeiten, bitte.
ts'oom ho-TEL feer YAHR-ess-ts'eye-ten, BIT-teh.

Excuse me, how can I go . . .
Verzeihung, wie komme ich . . .
fair-TS'Y-oong, vee KOHM-eh ikh . . .

. . . to the Hotel Kronprinzen?
. . . zum Hotel Kronprinzen?
. . . ts'oom ho-TEL KROHN-prin-ts'en?

. . . to a good restaurant?
. . . zu einem guten Restaurant?
. . . ts'oo INE-em GOOT-en rest-oh-RAHNG?

. . . to this address?
. . . zu dieser Adresse?
. . . ts'oo DEE-zer ah-DRES-seh?

. . . to the movies?
. . . zum Kino?
. . . ts'oom KEE-no?

. . . to the post office? . . . to a police station?
. . . zur Post?   . . . zur Polizeistation?
. . . ts'oor post?   . . . ts'oor po-lee-TS'Y-shta-ts'yohn?

. . . to a pharmacy?
. . . zur Apotheke?
. . . *ts'oor ah-po-TAYK-eh?*

. . . to a hospital?
. . . zu einem Krankenhaus?
. . . *ts'oo INE-em KRAHN-ken-howss?*

. . . to a barber? (or hairdresser)
. . . zu einem Friseur?
. . . *ts'oo INE-em free-ZERR?*

. . . to the American consulate?
. . . zum amerikanischen Konsulat?
. . . *ts'oom ah-meh-ree-KAHN-ee-shen kon-soo-LAHT?*

. . . Canadian . . .	. . . British . . .
. . . kanadischen . . .	. . . britischen . . .
. . . *kah-NA-dee-shen* . . .	. . . *BRIT-ee-shen* . . .

Follow this street to the Kaiser-Wilhelm Street.
Gehen Sie diese Straße bis zur Kaiser Wilhelm Straße.
GAY'en zee DEE-seh SHTRAHSS-eh bis ts'oor KI-zer
VIL-helm SHTRAHSS-eh.

Then right.	Left.	On the corner.
Dann rechts.	Links.	An der Ecke.
dahn rekhts.	*links.*	*ahn dair EK-eh.*

At Frederick Street turn left.
An der Friedrichstraße nach links.
ahn dair FREE-drikh-SHTRAHSS-eh nahkh links.

Is it far?	Quite far.
Ist es weit?	Ziemlich weit.
isst ess vite?	*TS'EEM-likh vite.*

---

1. Pronounce *ü* like "ee" with your lips in a tight circle.
2. *kh* is a guttural sound.
3. Stress the syllables in capital letters.

No. It is near.
Nein. Es ist nah.
nine. ess isst nah.

Thank you very much.   Very kind of you.
Danke vielmals.   Sehr nett von Ihnen.
DAHNK-eh FEEL-mahlss.   *zair net fohn EEN-en.*

When you speak to a stranger don't forget to say **Entschuldigung** followed by **mein Herr** to a man, **meine Dame** to a lady, or **Fräulein** to a young girl before you ask a question.

Streets in Germany, Austria, and Switzerland have signs attached to the buildings at each corner, making it easy to find out where you are.

To make sure you understand people's answers, you can show them the "Point to the Answer" sections of this book.

🦅 5. Hotel—Laundry—Dry Cleaning

Although the staffs of the larger hotels have some training in English, you will find that the use of German makes for better understanding and better relations, especially with the service personnel. We have included laundry and dry cleaning in this section as this is one of the things for which you have to make yourself understood in speaking to the hotel chambermaid or valet.

Can you recommend a good hotel?
Können Sie mir ein gutes Hotel empfehlen?
KERN'en zee meer ine GOOT-es ho-TEL emp-FAIL'en?

. . . a guest house?
. . . einen Gasthof?
. . . INE-en GAHST-hohf?

In the center of town?
Im Zentrum der Stadt.
im TS'EN-troom dair shtaht.

Not too expensive.
Nicht zu teuer.
nikht ts'oo TOY-er.

My name is ———
Mein Name ist ———
mine NA-meh isst ———

I've made a reservation.
Ich habe reservieren lassen.
ikh HAHB-eh reh-zer-VEER'en LAHSS'en.

Have you a room?
Haben Sie ein Zimmer?
HAHB'en zee ine TS'IM-er?

I would like . . .
Ich hätte gern . . .
ikh HET-teh gairn . . .

. . . a single room.
. . . ein Einzelzimmer.
. . . ine INE-ts'el-ts'im-er.

---

1. Pronounce *ü* like "ee" with your lips in a tight circle.
2. *kh* is a guttural sound.
3. Stress the syllables in capital letters.

... a double room.
... ein Doppelzimmer.
... *ine DOPP-el-ts'im-er.*

... with two beds.
... mit zwei Betten.
... *mit ts'vy BET-ten.*

... with a bath.
... mit Bad.
... *mit baht.*

... with hot water.
... mit heißem Wasser.
... *mit HI-sem VAHS-ser.*

... with a balcony.
... mit Balkon.
... *mit bahl-KOHN.*

... with a radio.
... mit einem Radio.
... *mit INE-em RAH-dee-oh.*

... with TV.
... mit Fernsehen.
... *mit FAIRN-zay'en.*

How much does it cost?
Wieviel kostet es?
vee-FEEL KO-stet ess?

... per day?
... pro Tag?
... *pro Tahk?*

... per week?
... pro Woche?
... *pro VO-kheh?*

Are the meals included?
Sind die Mahlzeiten ein-
    begriffen?
*zint dee MAHL-ts'y-ten
    INE-beh-griff'en?*

Is breakfast included?
Ist das Frühstück einbegriffen?
isst dahss FRÜ-shtůk INE-beh-griff'en?

I should like to see it.
Ich möchte das Zimmer sehen.
ikh MERKH-teh dahss TS'IM-er ZAY'en.

Where is the bath?
Wo ist das Bad?
voh isst dahss baht?

... the shower?
... das Brausebad?
... *dahss BROW-zeh-baht?*

I'd like another room.
Ich möchte ein anderes Zimmer haben.
ikh MERKH-teh ine AHN-der-ess TS'IM-er HAHB'en.

... **on a higher floor.**
... in einem höheren Stockwerk.
... *im INE-em HER-er-en SHTOCK-vehrk.*

... **better.**	... **larger.**	... **smaller.**
... besser.	... größer.	... kleiner.
... *BES-ser.*	... *GRERS-ser.*	... *KLINE-er.*

I'll take this.	**I'll stay for five days.**
Ich nehme dieses.	Ich bleibe fünf Tage.
ikh NAY-meh DEE-zes.	*ikh BLY-beh fünf TA-geh.*

About one week.
Ungefähr eine Woche.
OON-gheh-fair INE-eh VO-kheh.

At what time do you serve lunch?
Um wieviel Uhr servieren Sie das Mittagessen?
oom VEE-feel oor zer-VEER'en zee dahss MIT-tahk-ess'en?

At what time do you serve dinner?
Um wieviel Uhr servieren Sie das Abendessen?
oom VEE-feel oor zer-VEER'en zee dahss AH-bent-ess'en?

I would like ...	... **mineral**	... **some ice.**
Ich möchte ...	**water**	... etwas Eis
ikh MERKH-	... Seltzerwasser	... *ET-vahss ice.*
teh ...	... *ZEL-ts'er-*	
	vahs-ser	

Breakfast for Room 405.
Frühstück für Zimmer vierhundertfünf.
FRÜ-shtük für TS'IM-er FEER-hoon-dert-fünf.

Coffee, rolls and butter.
Kaffee, Brötchen und Butter.
KA-fay, BRERT-khen oont BOOT-ter.

---

1. Pronounce *ü* like "ee" with your lips in a tight circle.
2. *kh* is a guttural sound.
3. Stress the syllables in capital letters.

For a more complete choice of breakfast foods, see page 38.

Will you send these letters for me?
Würden Sie diese Briefe für mich abschicken?.
VÜR-den zee DEE-zeh BREE-feh für mikh AHP-shik'en?

Will you put stamps on them?
Würden Sie Marken aufkleben?
VÜR-den zee MAR-ken OWF-clay-ben?

My key please.
Meinen Schlüssel, bitte.
MY-nen SHLÜSS-el, BIT-teh.

Send my mail to this address.
Schicken Sie meine Post an diese Adresse.
SHIK'en zee MY-neh post ahn DEE-zeh ah-DRESS-eh.

Have you mail for me?
Haben Sie Post für mich?
HAHB'en zee post für mikh?

I want to speak to the manager.
Ich möchte den Direktor sprechen.
ikh MERKH-teh den dee-REK-tor SHPREKH'en.

I need an interpreter.
Ich brauche einen Dolmetscher.
ikh BROW-kheh INE-en DOHL-meh-cher.

Are you the chambermaid?
Sind Sie das Zimmermädchen?
zint zee dahss TS'IM-er-mayt-yen?

I need . . .	. . . a blanket.
Ich brauche . . .	. . . eine Decke.
ikh BROW-kheh . . .	*. . . INE-eh DEK-eh.*

... a pillow.
... ein Kissen.
... *ine KIS-sen.*

... soap.
... Seife.
... *ZY-feh.*

... a towel.
... ein Handtuch.
... *ine HAHNT-tookh.*

... toilet paper.
... Toilettenpapier.
... *twa-LET-ten-pa-peer.*

That is to be cleaned.
Das muß gereinigt werden.
dahss mooss ghe-RINE-nikht VAIRD'en.

That is to be pressed.
Das muß gebügelt werden.
dahss mooss ghe-BÜ-ghelt VAIRD'en.

That is to be washed.
Das muß gewaschen werden.
dahss mooss ghe-VA-shen VAIRD'en.

That is to be repaired.
Das muß repariert werden.
dahss mooss reh-pa-REERT VAIRD'en.

For this evening?
Für heute abend?
für HOY-teh AH-bent?

For ... tomorrow?
Für ... morgen?
für ... MOR-ghen?

... tomorrow afternoon?
... morgen nachmittag?
... *MOR-ghen NAKH-mit-tahk?*

... tomorrow evening?
... morgen abend?
... *MOR-ghen AH-bent?*

Be careful with this.
Seien Sie vorsichtig damit.
ZY'en zee FOR-zikh-tikh da-MIT.

When?
Wann?
vahn?

For sure?
Sicher?
ZIKH-er?

---

1. Pronounce *ü* like "ee" with your lips in a tight circle.
2. *kh* is a guttural sound.
3. Stress the syllables in capital letters.

Are my things ready?
Sind meine Sachen fertig?
zint MY-neh ZAHKH-en FAIR-tikh?

My bill, please.
Meine Rechnung, bitte.
MY-neh REKH-noon, BIT-teh.

I'm leaving tomorrow morning.
Ich reise morgen früh ab.
ikh RY-zeh MOR-ghen frü ahp.

Please call me at seven o'clock.
Bitte rufen Sie mich um sieben Uhr an.
BIT-teh ROOF'en zee mikh oom ZEE-ben oor ahn.

It's very important.
Es ist sehr wichtig.
ess isst zair VIKH-tikh.

Hotel floors are generally counted starting above the ground floor—**Erdgeschoß** or **Grundstock**—so that the second floor is called the first, the third the second, etc.

You never have to ask for a shoeshine. Just leave your shoes outside the door as you retire. Not a bad idea, **nicht wahr?** (isn't that true?)

Point to the Answer

Zeigen Sie bitte auf dieser Seite Ihre Antwort auf meine Frage. Danke.
Please point on this page to your answer to my question. Thank you.

Heute.	**Heute abend.**	**Morgen.**
Today.	This evening.	Tomorrow.

Früh.					Spät.
Early.					Late.

Vor ein,	zwei,	drei,	vier,	fünf,	sechs Uhr.
Before one,	two,	three,	four,	five,	six o'clock.

Um sieben,	acht,	neun,	zehn,	elf,	zwölf Uhr.
At seven,	eight,	nine,	ten,	eleven,	twelve o'clock.

Montag	Dienstag	Mittwoch	Donnerstag
Monday	Tuesday	Wednesday	Thursday

Freitag	Sonnabend	Sonntag
Friday	(Samstag)	Sunday
	Saturday	

🦅 6. Time: Hours—Days— Months

In the "Hotel" section you noted that when making an appointment at a certain hour you simply put um in front of the number followed by Uhr (hour). The following section shows you how to tell time in greater detail, including dates. You can make all sorts of arrangements with people by indicating the hour, the day, the date, and adding Einverstanden?—"Is it agreed?" or "OK?"

What time is it?	It is one o'clock.	It is six o'clock.
Wie spät ist es?	Es ist ein Uhr.	Es ist sechs Uhr.
vee shpayt isst ess?	*ess isst ine oor.*	*ess ist zex oor.*

six thirty (or) half-past six
sechs Uhr dreißig (or) halb sieben
zex oor DRY-sikh   hahlp ZEE-ben

a quarter past seven	a quarter to eight
viertel nach sieben	viertel vor acht
FEER-tel nahkh ZEE-ben	*FEER-tel for ahkht*

ten minutes past ten
zehn Minuten nach zehn
ts'ayn mee-NOOT-en nahkh ts'ayn

ten minutes to three	at nine o'clock
zehn Minuten vor drei	um neun Uhr
ts'ayn mee-NOOT-en for dry	*oom noyn oor*

exactly nine o'clock	the morning
punkt neun Uhr	der Morgen
poonkt noyn oor	*dair MOR-ghen*

noon	the afternoon
der Mittag	der Nachmittag
dair MIT-tahk	*dair NAKH- mit-tahk*

the evening
der Abend
dair AH-bent

the night
die Nacht
dee nakht

today
heute
HOY-teh

yesterday
gestern
GUESS-tern

the day before yesterday
vorgestern
FOR-guess-tern

tomorrow
morgen
MOR-ghen

the day after tomorrow
übermorgen
Ü-BER-mor-ghen

this morning
heute Morgen
HOY-teh MOR-ghen

tomorrow morning
morgen früh
MOR-ghen frü

this evening
heute Abend
HOY-teh AH-bent

tomorrow evening
morgen Abend
MOR-ghen AH-bent

last night
gestern Abend
GUESS-tern AH-bent

our last evening here
unser letzter Abend hier
OON-zer LET-ster AH-bent heer

this week
diese Woche
DEE-zeh VO-kheh

last week
vorige Woche
FOR-ig-eh VO-kheh

next week
nächste Woche
NAIK-steh VO-kheh

two weeks ago
vor zwei Wochen
for ts'vy VO-khen

this month
diesen Monat
DEE-zen MO-naht

next month
nächsten Monat
NAYK-sten MO-naht

---

1. Pronounce *ü* like "ee" with your lips in a tight circle.
2. *kh* is a guttural sound.
3. Stress the syllables in capital letters.

several months ago
vor einigen Monaten
for INE-ig-en MO-naht-en

this year
dieses Jahr
DEE-zes yar

last year
voriges Jahr
FOR-ig-ess yar

next year
nächstes Jahr
NAIK-stehs yar

five years ago
vor fünf Jahren
for fünf YAR-en

1970
neunzehnhundertsiebzig
NOYN-ts'ayn-hoon-dert-ZEEP-ts'ikh

Monday
Montag
MOHN-tahk

Tuesday
Dienstag
DEENSS-tahk

Wednesday
Mittwoch
MIT-vohkh

Thursday
Donnerstag
DOH-nerss-tahk

Friday
Freitag
FRY-tahk

Saturday
Samstag (or) Sonnabend
ZAHMSS-tahk ZOHN-ah-bent

Sunday
Sonntag
ZOHN-tahk

next Monday
nächsten Montag
NAYK-sten MOHN-tahk

last Tuesday
vorigen Dienstag
FOR-ig-en DEENSS-tahk

on Fridays
Freitags
FRY-tahks

January
Januar
YA-noo-ar

February
Februar
FEB-roo-ar

March
März
mairts

April
April
ah-PREEL

May
Mai
my

June
Juni
YOO-nee

July
Juli
YOO-lee

August
August ·
ow-GOOST

September
September
zep-TEM-ber

October	November	December
Oktober	November	Dezember
ohk-TOH-ber	*no-VEM-ber*	*day-TS'EM-ber*

What date?
Welches Datum?
VEL-khess DA-toom?

on the first of March
am ersten März
ahm AIR-sten mairts

on the second ...
am zweiten ...
ahm TS'VY-ten ...

third ...
dritten ...
DRIT-ten ...

fourth of March.
vierten März.
FEER-ten mairts.

the 25th of December
am fünfundzwanzigsten
  Dezember
ahm fûnf-oont-TS'VAHN-
  ts'ikh-sten
  day-TS'EM-ber

Merry Christmas!
Fröhliche Weihnachten!
FRER-likh-eh
  VY-nahkh-ten!

on the first of January
am ersten Januar
ahm AIR-sten YA-noo-ar

Happy New Year!
Glückliches Neujahr!
GLÜKH-likh-ess NOY-yar!

Today is a holiday.
Heute ist ein Feiertag.
HOY-teh isst ine FY-er-takh.

---

1. Pronounce *û* like "ee" with your lips in a tight circle.
2. *kh* is a guttural sound.
3. Stress the syllables in capital letters.

 # 7. Money

This section contains the vocabulary necessary for changing money. The written abbreviation for the German mark is **DM.**, for the Austrian schilling **Sch.**, and for the Swiss franc **Fr.**

Where can I change money?
Wo kann ich Geld umtauschen?
vo kahn ikh ghelt OOM-t'ow-shen?

Can I change dollars here?
Kann ich hier Dollar umtauschen?
kahn ikh heer DOH-lar OOM-t'ow-shen?

Where is the moneychanger?
Wo ist der Geldwechsler?
vo isst dair GHELT-vex-ler?

Where is the bank?
Wo ist die Bank?
vo isst dee bahnk?

What time does the bank open?
Um wieviel Uhr öffnet die Bank?
oom VEE-feel oor ERF-net dee bahnk?

When does the bank close?
Wann schließt die Bank?
vahnn shleest dee bahnk?

What is the dollar rate?
Was ist der Dollarwert?
vahss isst dair DOH-lar-vairt?

It is four marks for one dollar.
Es ist vier Mark auf einen Dollar.
ess isst feer mark owf INE-en DOH-lar.

I want to change $50.
Ich möchte fünfzig Dollar wechseln.
ikh MERKH-teh FÜNF-ts'ikh DOH-lar VEX-eln.

Do you accept traveler's checks?
Nehmen Sie Reiseschecks?
NAYM'en zee RYE-zeh-sheks?

Of course.
Natürlich.
na-TÜR-likh.

Unfortunately not.
Leider nicht.
LY-der nikht.

Will you accept my check?
Nehmen Sie meinen Scheck?
NAYM'en zee MY-nen shek?

Have you identification with you?
Haben Sie einen Ausweis bei sich?
HAHB'en zee INE-en OWSS-vice by zikh?

Yes indeed.
Jawohl.
ya-VOHL.

Here is my passport.
Hier ist mein Pass.
heer isst mine pahss.

Give me two fifty-mark notes.
Geben Sie mir zwei Fünfzigmarkscheine.
GAYB'en zee meer ts'vy FÜNF-ts'ikh-mark-shy-neh.

I need some small change.
Ich brauche Kleingeld.
ikh BROW-kheh KLINE-ghelt.

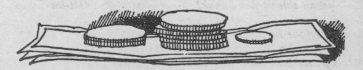

---

1. Pronounce *ü* like "ee" with your lips in a tight circle.
2. *kh* is a guttural sound.
3. Stress the syllables in capital letters.

# 8. Basic Foods

The foods and drinks mentioned in this section will enable you to be well-fed in your travels in German-speaking countries. The section that follows this will deal with special regional dishes, representative of the tasty and substantial cuisine of Germany and Austria.

breakfast
das Frühstück
dahss FRÜ-shtŭk

orange juice
Orangensaft
oh-RAHN-ghen-zahft

boiled eggs
gekochte Eier
ghe-KOKH-teh EYE-er

fried eggs
Spiegeleier
SHPEE-ghel-eye-er

with bacon
mit Speck
mit shpeck

with ham
mit Schinken
mit SHINK-en

an omelet
ein Omelett
ine ohm-LET

scrambled eggs
Rühreier
RÜR-eye-er

toast
Toast
toast

coffee with cream
Kaffee mit Sahne
ka-FAY mit ZA-neh

coffee with hot milk
Kaffee mit heißer Milch
ka-FAY mit HY-ser milkh

hot chocolate
heiße Schokolade
HI-seh sho-ko-LA-deh

tea with lemon
Tee mit Zitrone
teh mit ts'ee-TRO-neh

lunch
Mittagessen
MIT-tahk-ess-en

dinner
Abendessen
AH-bent-ess-en

Do you know a good restaurant?
Kennen Sie ein gutes Restaurant?
KEN'en zee ine GOOT-es reh-sto-RAHNG?

A table for three.
Ein Tisch für drei.
ine tish für dry.

Follow me, please.
Folgen Sie mir, bitte.
FOLG'en zee meer, BIT-teh.

The menu, please.
Die Speisekarte, bitte.
dee SHPY-zeh-car-teh, BIT-teh.

What do you recommend?
Was können Sie empfehlen?
vahss KERN'en zee emp-FAIL'en?

What is this?
Was ist das?
vahss isst dahss?

I'll take this.
Ich nehme das.
ikh NAY-meh dahss.

First a cocktail.
Zuerst einen Cocktail.
ts'oo-EHRST INE-en cocktail.

Then an appetizer.
Dann eine Vorspeise.
dahn INE-eh FOR-shpy-zeh.

herring	salmon	oysters
Hering	Lachs	Austern
HEHR-ring	*lahx*	*OWS-tern*

lobster	soup	fish
Hummer	Suppe	Fisch
HOOM-mer	*ZOOP-peh*	*fish*

chicken	roast chicken	duck
Hühnchen	Hühnerbraten	Ente
HÜNT-yen	*HÜ-ner-bra-ten*	*EN-teh*

---

1. Pronounce *ü* like "ee" with your lips in a tight circle.
2. *kh* is a guttural sound.
3. Stress the syllables in capital letters.

pork	lamb	roast veal
Schweinefleisch	Lammfleisch	Kalbsbraten
SHVY-neh-flysh	*LAHM-flysh*	*KAHLPS-bra-ten*

sausage (big)	sausage (small)	chopped steak
Wurst	Würstchen	Hackbraten
voorst	*VÜRST-yen*	*HAHK-bra-ten*

steak	rare	well done	bread
Steak	roh	gut durchgebraten	Brot
shtehk	*ro*	*goot DOORKH-ghe-braht'en*	*broht*

butter	noodles	without ...	with ...
Butter	Nudeln	ohne ...	mit ...
BOOT-ter	*NOO-deln*	*OH-neh ...*	*mit ...*

vegetables	rice	green beans
Gemüse	Reis	grüne Bohnen
ghe-MÜ-zeh	*rice*	*GRÜ-neh BO-nen*

peas	spinach	carrots
Erbsen	Spinat	Karotten
ERP-sen	*shpin-AHT*	*ka-ROHT-ten*

cabbage	tomatoes	onions
Kohl	Tomaten	Zwiebeln
kohl	*toh-MA-ten*	*TS'VEE-beln*

mushrooms	asparagus	garlic
Pilze	Spargel	Knoblauch
PIL-ts'eh	*SHPAR-ghel*	*K'NOB-l'owkh*

fried potatoes	boiled potatoes	mashed potatoes
Bratkartoffeln	Salzkartoffeln	Kartoffelpüree
BRAHT-kar-toff-eln	*ZAHLTS-kar-toff-eln*	*kar-TOFF-el-pü ray*

potato salad	salad	oil
Kartoffelsalat	Salat	Öl
kar-TOFF-el-za-laht	*za-LAHT*	*erl*

vinegar	salt	pepper	mustard
Essig	Salz	Pfeffer	Senf
ESS-ikh	*zahlts*	*PFEF-er*	*zenf*

What wine do you recommend?
Welchen Wein empfehlen Sie?
VEL-khen vine emp-FAIL'en zee?

white wine	red wine
Weißwein	Rotwein
VICE-vine	*ROHT-vine*

beer	light beer	dark beer
Bier	helles Bier	dunkles Bier
beer	*HELL-ess beer*	*DOONK-less beer*

champagne	To your health!
Sekt	Prosit!
zekt	*PRO-zit!*

fruit	grapes	peaches
Obst	Weintrauben	Pfirsiche
ohpst	*VINE-tr'ow-ben*	*PFEER-zikh-eh*

apples	pears	bananas
Äpfel	Birnen	Bananen
EHP-fel	*BEER-nen*	*ba-NA-nen*

pineapples	strawberries	oranges
Ananas	Erdbeeren	Apfelsinen
ah-na-NAHSS	*AIRD-bair-en*	*ahp-fel-ZEE-nen*

---

1. Pronounce *ü* like "ee" with your lips in a tight circle.
2. *kh* is a guttural sound.
3. Stress the syllables in capital letters.

For dessert:	cake	pastry	cheese
Zum Nachtisch:	Kuchen	Gebäck	Käse
ts'oom NAHKH-tish	*KOO-khen*	*ghe-BAKE*	*KAY-zeh*

ice cream	coffee	expresso
Eiscreme	Kaffee	Expresso
ICE-kreh-meh	*ka-FAY*	*expresso*

More, please.	That's enough, thank you.
Mehr, bitte.	Das ist genug, danke.
mair, BIT-teh.	*dahss isst ghe-NOOK, DAHN-keh.*

Waiter!	Waitress!	The check, please.
Herr Ober!	Fräulein!	Die Rechnung, bitte.
hair OH-ber!	*FROY-line!*	*dee REKH-noong, BIT-teh.*

Is the tip included?
Ist das Trinkgeld einbegriffen?
isst dahss TRINK-ghelt INE-beh-griff'en?

I think the bill is incorrect.
Ich glaube, die Rechnung stimmt nicht.
ikh GL'OW-beh, dee REKH-noong shtimt nikht.

Oh no, sir ...	look here ...	... you see?
Aber nein, mein	schauen Sie	... sehen Sie?
Herr ...	her ...	... ZAY'en zee?
AH-ber nine,	*SH'OW'en zee*	
mine hair ...	*hair ...*	

Yes, that's right.	It's O.K.
Ja, das ist richtig.	Das ist in Ordnung.
ya, dahss isst RIKH-tikh.	*dahss isst in ORD-noong.*

Come again soon.
Kommen Sie bald wieder.
KOHM'en zee bahlt VEE-der.

Point to the Answer

Zeigen Sie bitte auf diéser Seite Ihre Antwort auf meine
   Frage. Danke.
Please point on this page to your answer to my question.
   Thank you.

Dies ist unser Spezialität.   Es ist fertig.
This is our specialty.   It's ready.

Es ist nicht fertig.   Es dauert ——— Minuten.
It isn't ready.   It takes ——— minutes.

Wir haben das heute nicht.   Es wird nur Freitags ser-
We don't have it today.   viert.
                                 It is served only on Fridays.

Es ist   Hühnchen,   Schweinefleisch,
It is   chicken,   pork,

Lammfleisch,   Kalbfleisch,   Rindfleisch,
lamb,   veal,   beef,

Wurst,   Fisch.
sausage,   fish.

... mit Gemüsen.   ... mit einer Soße.
... with vegetables.   ... with a sauce.

---

1. Pronounce *ŭ* like "ee" with your lips in a tight circle.
2. *kh* is a guttural sound.
3. Stress the syllables in capital letters.

🦅 9. Food Specialties of Germany and Austria

Knowing the names of special dishes will be useful in restaurants or private homes where you may be invited. These dishes commonly appear on most German menus and are so much a part of German and Austrian dining tradition that you should recognize them and know how to pronounce them as well as to enjoy them. We have written the German first, since this is how you will see it on the menu.

Gulaschsuppe
GOO-lahsh ZOOP-eh
veal soup with spices

Ochsenschwanzsuppe
OX-en-shvahnts-zoop-eh
oxtail soup

Gemischter Aufschnitt
ghe-MISH-ter OWF-shnit
mixed cold cuts

Gekochte Rinderbrust
ghe-KOHK-teh RIN-der-broost
boiled brisket of beef

Hasenpfeffer
HA-zen-pfef-er
rabbit stewed in vinegar and pepper

Schweinepfeffer mit Knödeln
SHVINE-eh-pfef-er mit K'NER-deln
spiced pork with dumplings

Rippchen mit Sauerkraut
RIP-khen mit Z'OW-er-kr'owt
pork chops with sauerkraut

Bauernschmaus
B'OW-ern-shm'owss
smoked ham, sausages, pork, and dumplings with sauerkraut

Sauerbraten mit Rotkohl
Z'OW-er-bra-ten mit ROHT-kohl
pot roast with red cabbage

Eintopfgericht
INE-tohpf-ghe-rikht
casserole of meat and vegetables

Nierenbraten
NEER-en-bra-ten
roast loin of veal with kidneys

Schweinebraten
SH'VY-neh-bra-ten
roast pork

Würstelbraten
VÜR-stel-bra-ten
roast beef with sausages

Geräucherter Rheinlachs
ghe-ROY-kher-ter RINE-lahx
smoked salmon from the Rhine

Sülze
ZÜL-ts'eh
meat in aspic

Blutwurst
BLOOT-voorst
blood sausage

Leberwurst
LAY-ber-voorst
liver sausage

Bratwurst
BRAHT-voorst
pork sausage

Wiener Würstchen
VEE-ner VÜRST-yen
"hot dogs"

Weißwurst
VICE-voorst
white veal sausage

Kartoffelpuffer
kar-TOFF-el-poof-er
potato pancakes

Lebkuchen
LAIP-koo-khen
spice cake

Doboschtorte
DOH-bosh-tort-eh
seven-layer cake with mocha cream

---

1. Pronounce *ü* like "ee" with your lips in a tight circle.
2. *kh* is a guttural sound.
3. Stress the syllables in capital letters.

Sachertorte
ZA-kher-tort-eh
chocolate cake
with whipped cream

How do you like it?
Wie schmeckt es Ihnen?
vee shmekt ess EEN-en?

It's delicious!
Es ist sehr schmackhaft!
ess isst zair SHMAHK-hahft!

It's excellent!
Ausgezeichnet!
OWSS-ghe-ts'eye-khnet!

My congratulations to the chef!
Ich gratuliere dem Koch!
ikh grah-too-LEER-eh dem kohkh!

Thank you for a wonderful dinner.
Danke sehr für ein wunderbares Abendessen!
DAHN-keh zair für ine voon-der-BAR-ess AH-bent-ess'en!

You are welcome.
Bitte schön.
BIT-teh shern.

I'm happy you enjoyed it.
Es freut mich, dass es Ihnen geschmeckt hat.
ess froyt mikh, dahss ess EEN-en ghe-shmehkt haht.

🦅 10. Transportation

Getting around by public transportation is enjoyable not only for the new and interesting things you see, but also because of the opportunities you have for practicing German. To make your travels easier, use short phrases when speaking to drivers or others when you ask directions. And don't forget **Bitte** and **Danke!**

Bus

Bus
Autobus
OW-toh-booss

Where is the bus stop?
Wo ist die Bushaltestelle?
vo isst dee BOOSS-hahl-teh-shtel-leh?

Do you go to the Railroad Terminal Square?
Fahren Sie zum Bahnhofplatz?
FAR'en zee ts'oom BAHN-hohf-plahtz?

No. Take number nine.
Nein. Nehmen Sie die Nummer neun.
nine. NAYM'en zee dee NOOM-er noyn.

How much is the fare?
Was kostet die Fahrt?
vahss KO-stet dee fahrt?

Where do you want to go?
Wo wollen Sie hin?
vo VOHL'en zee hin?

To the cathedral.
Zum Dom.
ts'oom dohm.

Is it far?
Ist es weit?
isst ess vite?

---

1. Pronounce *ü* like "ee" with your lips in a tight circle.
2. *kh* is a guttural sound.
3. Stress the syllables in capital letters.

No. It's near.
Nein. Es ist in der Nähe.
nine. ess isst in dair NAY-eh.

Please tell me where to get off.
Bitte sagen Sie mir, wo ich aussteigen muß.
BIT-teh ZAHG'en zee meer, vo ikh OWSS-shtyg'en mooss.

Get off here.
Steigen Sie hier aus.
SHTYG'en zee heer OWSS.

Point to the Answer

Zeigen Sie bitte auf dieser Seite Ihre Antwort auf meine Frage. Danke.
Please point on this page to your answer to my question. Thank you.

Dort drüben.	**In dieser Richtung.**	**Ich weiß nicht.**
Over there.	In this direction.	I don't know.

Auf der anderen Seite der Straße.	**An der Ecke.**
On the other side of the street.	At the corner.

Nach rechts.	**Nach links.**	**Immer geradeaus.**
To the right.	To the left.	Straight ahead.

Taxi

Taxi!	**Are you free?**
Taxi!	Sind Sie frei?
tahk-see!	*zint zee fry?*

Where to?	**To this address.**
Wohin?	Zu dieser Adresse.
vo-HIN?	*ts'oo DEE-zer ah-DRESS- eh.*

Do you know where it is?
Wissen Sie, wo das ist?
VISS'en zee, vo dahss isst?

I am in a hurry.
Ich bin in Eile.
ikh bin in EYE-leh.

Go fast!
Fahren Sie schnell!
FAR'en zee shnell!

Slow down!
Fahren Sie langsamer!
*FAR'en zee LAHNG-zah-
    mer!*

Stop here.
Halten Sie hier.
HAHLT'en zee heer.

At the corner.
An der Ecke.
ahn dair EHK-eh.

Wait for me.
Warten Sie auf mich.
VART'en zee owf mikh.

I can't park here.
Ich kann hier nicht parken.
*Ikh kahn heer nikht
    PARK'en.*

I'll be back soon.
Ich komme gleich zurück.
*Ikh KOHM-eh glykh
    ts'oo-RÜK.*

In five minutes.
In fünf Minuten.
in fünf mee-NOOT-en.

O.K.!
Einverstanden!
INE-fair-shtahn-den!

I'll wait.
Ich werde warten.
ikh VAIR-deh vart'en.

How much is it per hour?
Was kostet es pro Stunde?
*vahss KO-stet ess pro
    SHTOON-deh?*

. . . per kilometer?
. . . der Kilometer?
. . . dair kee-lo-MAYT-er?

---

1. Pronounce *ü* like "ee" with your lips in a tight circle.
2. *kh* is a guttural sound.
3. Stress the syllables in capital letters.

Come again tomorrow.
Kommen Sie morgen wieder.
KOHM'en zee MOR-ghen VEE-der.

In the morning.	**In the afternoon.**
Am Vormittag.	Am Nachmittag.
ahm FOR-mit-tahk.	*ahm NAHKH-mit-tahk.*

At three o'clock.	**At the Hotel National.**
Um drei Uhr.	Im Hotel National.
oom dry oor.	*im ho-TEL na-ts'yo-NAHL.*

Tip 10 percent or 15 percent of the meter. After midnight there is a surcharge.

Point to the Answer

Zeigen Sie bitte auf dieser Seite Ihre Antwort auf meine Frage. Danke.
Please point on this page to your answer to my question. Thank you.

Ich warte auf Sie hier.
I will wait for you here.

Ich kann nicht warten.
I can't wait.

Ich komme zurück um Sie abzuholen.
I'll be back to pick you up.

Das ist nicht genug.	**Das Gepäck ist extra.**
It's not enough.	The baggage is extra.

Subway

subway
U-Bahn (Untergrundbahn)
OO-bahn (OON-ter-groont-bahn)

Is there a subway in this city?
Gibt es in dieser Stadt eine U-Bahn?
ghipt ess in DEE-zer shtaht INE-eh OO-bahn?

Where is the subway?
Wo ist die U-Bahn?
vo isst dee OO-bahn?

U-Bahn is short for Untergrundbahn—"underground
railroad."

Train

Where is the railroad station?
Wo ist der Bahnhof?
vo isst dair BAHN-hohf?

Where do I buy tickets?
Wo kann ich Fahrkarten kaufen?
vo kahn ikh FAR-kar-ten KOW-fen?

One ticket for Munich.
Eine Fahrkarte nach München.
INE-eh FAR-kar-teh nahkh MÜNT-yen.

Round trip.	**One way.**	**A timetable.**
Hin- und Rückfahrt.	Nur einfach.	Ein Fahrplan.
hin oont RÜK-fahrt.	*noor INE-fakh.*	*ine FAR-plahn.*

---

1. Pronounce *ü* like "ee" with your lips in a tight circle.
2. *kh* is a guttural sound.
3. Stress the syllables in capital letters.

First class.   **Second class.**
Erste Klasse.   Zweite Klasse.
EHRST-eh KLAHSS-eh.   *TS'VY-teh KLAHSS-eh.*

Where is the train for Cologne?
Wo ist der Zug nach Köln?
vo isst der ts'ook nakh Kerln?

When do we leave?   **Is this seat taken?**
Wann fahren wir ab?   Ist dieser Platz besetzt?
vahn FAR'en veer ahp?   *isst DEE-zer plahts beh-*
                                         ZETST?

With your permission.   **Of course.**
Erlauben Sie, bitte.   Natürlich.
air-L'OW-ben zee, BIT-teh.   *na-TÜR-likh.*

At what time do we arrive in Hamburg?
Um wieviel Uhr kommen wir in Hamburg an?
oom VEE-feel oor KOHM'en veer in HAHM-boorg ahn?

Does the train stop in Bremen?
Hält der Zug in Bremen?
hehlt dair ts'ook in BRAY-men?

How long does the train stop here?
Wie lange hält der Zug hier?
vee LAHNG-eh hehlt dair ts'ook heer?

Where is the dining car?
Wo ist der Speisewagen?
vo isst dair SHPY-zeh-va-ghen?

I can't find my ticket.
Ich kann meine Fahrkarte nicht finden.
ikh kahn MINE-eh FAR-kar-teh nikht FIN-den.

Wait.   **Here it is.**
Warten Sie.   Hier ist sie.
VART'en zee.   *heer isst zee.*

Can you help me?
Können Sie mir helfen?
KERN'en zee meer HELF'en?

I took the wrong train.
Ich habe nicht den richtigen Zug genommen.
ikh HAHB-eh nikht den RIKH-tee-ghen ts'ook ghe-NOHM'en.

I'd like to go to Berlin.
Ich möchte gern nach Berlin fahren.
ikh MERKH-teh gairn nakh bair-LEEN FAR'en.

Point to the Answer

Zeigen Sie bitte auf dieser Seite Ihre Antwort auf meine Frage. Danke.
Please point on this page to your answer to my question. Thank you.

Bahnsteig Nummer ———.
Track number ———.

Unten.   **Oben.**   **In dieser Richtung.**
Downstairs.   Upstairs.   That way.

Der Zug geht in ——— Minuten.
The train leaves in ——— minutes.

Dies ist nicht Ihr Zug.   **Er geht nach ———.**
This is not your train.   It goes to ———.

Sie müssen in ——— umsteigen.
You must change at ———.

---

1. Pronounce *ü* like "ee" with your lips in a tight circle.
2. *kh* is a guttural sound.
3. Stress the syllables in capital letters.

Wir kommen um ——— Uhr an.
We arrive at ——— o'clock.

Ship

What time does the ship sail?
Um wieviel Uhr fahrt das Schiff ab?
oom VEE-feel oor fahrt dahss shif ahp?

From which pier?
Von welcher Anlegestelle?
fohn VEL-kher AHN-leh-ghe-shtel-eh?

Where is my cabin?
Wo ist meine Kabine?
vo isst MINE-eh ka-BEE-neh?

Where is my luggage?   **... the purser?**
Wo ist mein Gepäck?   ... der Zahlmeister?
vo isst mine ghe-PAYK?   *... dair TS'AHL-my-ster?*

Where is ...   **... the swimming pool?**   **... the bar?**
Wo ist ...   ... das Schwimmbad?   ... die Bar?
vo isst ...   *... dahss SHVIM-baht?*   *... dee bar?*

... the movie?   **... the dining salon?**
... das Kino?   ... der Speisesaal?
... dahss KEE-no?   *... dair SHPY-zeh-zahl?*

yacht	**launch**	**sail boat**
Jacht	Barkasse	Segelboot
yahkht	*BAR-kas-seh*	*ZEH-ghel-boat*

first class	**tourist class**
erste Klasse	Touristenklasse
EHRST-eh KLAHSS-eh	*too-RIST-en-klahss-eh*

ferry	**Rhine steamboat**
Fähre	Rheindampfer
FAIR-eh	*RINE-dahmp-fer.*

🦅 11. Trips by Car

Car Rental

Where can one rent a car?
Wo kann man einen Wagen mieten?
vo kahn mahn INE-en VA-ghen MEET'en?

Where can one ...   ... rent a motorcycle?
Wo kann man ...   ... ein Motorrad mieten?
vo kahn mahn ...   ... ine MO-tohr-raht MEET'en?

... rent a bicycle?
... ein Fahrrad mieten?
... ine FAR-raht MEET'en?

I want to rent a car.
Ich möchte einen Wagen mieten.
ikh MERKH-teh INE-en VA-ghen MEET'en.

How much per day?
Wieviel kostet es pro Tag?
vee-FEEL KO-stet ess pro tahk?

How much per kilometer? *
Wieviel pro Kilometer?
vee-FEEL pro kee-lo-MAYT-er?

   * Distances are reckoned in kilometers, approximately ⅝ of a mile.

Is the gasoline included?
Ist Benzin mit einbegriffen?
isst ben-TS'EEN mit INE-beh-griff'en?

---

1. Pronounce *ü* like "ee" with your lips in a tight circle.
2. *kh* is a guttural sound.
3. Stress the syllables in capital letters.

Is the transmission automatic?
Hat der Wagen eine automatische Schaltung?
haht der VA-ghen INE-eh ow-toh-MA-tish-eh
    SHAHL-toong?

I would like to try it out.
Ich würde ihn gerne ausprobieren.
ikh VÜR-deh een GAIRN-eh OWSS-pro-beer'en.

Gas Station

Where is the next gas station?
Wo ist die nächste Tankstelle?
vo isst dee NAIKH-steh TAHNK-shtel-eh?

How much per liter? *
Was kostet der Liter?
vahss KO-stet dair LEE-ter?

    * Gas is sold by the liter—1.05 quarts; four liters make
approximately one gallon.

Thirty liters, please.
Dreißig Liter, bitte.
DRY-sikh LEE-ter, BIT-teh.

Fill up the tank.
Machen Sie den Tank voll.
MAHKH'en zee den tahnk fohl.

Please check whether . . .   **. . . the tires . . .**
Bitte sehen Sie nach, ob . . .   . . . die Reifen . . .
BIT-teh ZAY'en zee nahkh,   *. . . dee RYE-fen . . .*
    ohp . . .

. . . the sparkplugs . . .   **. . . the brakes . . .**
. . . die Zündkerzen . . .   . . . die Bremsen . . .
. . . dee TS'ÜNT-kair-ts'en . . .   *. . . dee BREM-zen . . .*

... are O.K.
... in Ordnung sind.
... *in ORD-noong zint.*

Please check whether ...   ... the water ...
Bitte sehen Sie nach, ob ...   ... das Wasser ...
BIT-teh ZAY'en zee nakhk,   ... *dahss VAHSS-er* ...
   ohp ...

... the oil ...   ... the carburetor ...
... das Öl ...   ... der Vergaser ...
... *dahss erl* ...   ... *dair fair-GA-zer* ...

... the battery ...   ... is O.K.
... die Batterie ...   ... in Ordnung ist.
... *dee ba-teh-REE* ...   ... *in ORD-noong isst.*

Change the oil, please.   Change this tire.
Ölwechsel, bitte.   Wechseln Sie diesen Reifen.
ERL-vex-el, BIT-teh.   *VEX-eln zee DEE-zen*
                                   RYE-fen.

The car needs a grease job.
Der Wagen braucht Schmierung.
dair VA-ghen browkht SHMEER-oong.

Wash the car.
Waschen Sie den Wagen.
VA-shen zee den VA-ghen.

A road map, please.
Eine Straßenkarte, bitte.
INE-eh SHTRA-sen-kar-teh, BIT-teh.

---

1. Pronounce *ü* like "ee" with your lips in a tight circle.
2. *kh* is a guttural sound.
3. Stress the syllables in capital letters.

Asking Directions

Where does this road lead?
Wohin führt diese Straße?
vo-HIN fŭrt DEE-zeh SHTRAHSS-eh?

Is this the way to Frankfurt?
Geht es hier nach Frankfurt?
gayt ess heer nakh FRAHNK-foort?

Is the road good?
Ist die Straße gut?
isst dee SHTRAHSS-eh goot?

Which is the highway to Stuttgart?
Welche Autobahn führt nach Stuttgart?
VEL-kheh OW-toh-bahn fŭrt nakh SHTOOT-gart?

In this direction.	**Is the next town far?**
In dieser Richtung.	Ist die nächste Stadt weit?
in DEE-zer RIKH-toong.	*isst dee NAYK-steh shtaht vite?*

Do you know a good restaurant there?
Kennen Sie ein gutes Restaurant dort?
KEN'en zee ine GOOT-es rest-oh-RAHNG dort?

Is there a good hotel in Mainz?
Gibt es ein gutes Hotel in Mainz?
ghipt ess ine GOOT-es ho-TEL in mine'ts?

Yes, there is a very good one.
Ja, es gibt ein sehr gutes.
ya, ess ghipt ine zair GOOT-es.

Fairly good.	**Is it far?**	**I don't know.**
Ziemlich gut.	Ist es weit?	Ich weiß nicht.
TS'EEM-likh goot.	*isst ess vite?*	*ikh vice nikht.*

About fifty kilometers.
Ungefähr fünfzig Kilometer.
OON-ghe-fair FÜNF-ts'ikh kee-lo-MAYT-er.

Stay on this road.
Bleiben Sie auf dieser Straße.
BLY-ben zee owf DEE-zer SHTRAHSS-eh.

Turn right as you leave the village.
Biegen Sie rechts ab am Ortsausgang.
BEE-ghen zee rekhts ahp ahm OHRTS-owss-gahng.

When you come to the bridge . . .
Wenn Sie zur Brücke kommen . . .
venn zee ts'oor BRÜK-eh KOHM'en . . .

you cross it . . .	**. . . and turn left.**
überqueren Sie sie . . .	. . . und biegen links ab.
über-K'VAIR'en zee zee . . .	*. . . oon BEE-ghen links ahp.*

Keep going straight ahead.
Immer geradeaus.
IM-mer ghe-RA-deh-owss.

The road is not bad.
Die Straße ist nicht schlecht.
dee SHTRAHSS-eh isst nikht shlekht.

Then go on the Autobahn.
Dann fahren Sie auf der Autobahn.
dahn FAR'en zee owf dair OW-toh-bahn.

---

1. Pronounce *ü* like "ee" with your lips in a tight circle.
2. *kh* is a guttural sound.
3. Stress the syllables in capital letters.

Point to the Answer

Zeigen Sie bitte auf dieser Seite Ihre Antwort auf meine Frage. Danke.
Please point on this page to your answer to my question. Thank you.

Gehen Sie nach rechts.
Go to the right.

Gehen Sie nach links.
Go to the left.

Gehen Sie immer geradeaus.
Go straight ahead.

. . . bis . . .
. . . until . . .

An der Verkehrsampel . . .
At the traffic light . . .

Sie sind hier auf der Karte.
You are here on the map.

Folgen Sie dieser Straße.
Follow this road.

Die nächste Stadt heißt ———.
The next town is called ———.

Emergencies and Repairs

Your license, please!
Ihren Führerschein, bitte!
EER-en FÜR-air-shine, BIT-teh!

Here it is, sir.
Hier ist er, mein Herr.
heer isst air, mine hair.

And the car registration.
Und die Kraftfahrkarte.
oont dee KRAHFT-far-kar-teh.

It wasn't my fault.
Es war nicht meine Schuld.
ess var nikht MINE-eh schoolt.

The truck skidded.
Der Lastwagen kam ins Schleudern.
wair LAHST-va-ghen kahm ins SHLOY-dern.

This fool crashed into me!
Dieser Dummkopf fuhr in mich hinein!
DEE-zer DOOM-kopf foor mikh hin-INE!

As German drivers are inclined to be rather competitive
—and fast—words like **Dummkopf!** (literally, "dumb-
head"), **Ochse!** ("ox"), **Idiot!**, etc., are frequent and rather
mild expletives. However, self-control and good humor,
plus a diplomatic use of German, will make driving safe
and enjoyable.

I am having difficulties.
Ich habe Schwierigkeiten.
ikh HAHB-eh SHVEE-rikh-kite-en.

My car has broken down.
Mein Wagen ist kaputt.
mine VA-ghen isst ka-POOT.

Can you help me?
Können Sie mir helfen?
KERN'en zee meer HELF'en?

I have a flat tire.
Ich habe eine Panne.
ikh HAHB-eh INE-eh PA-neh.

Can you lend me a jack?
Können Sie mir einen Wagenheber leihen?
KERN'en zee meer INE-en VA-ghen-hay-ber LIE'en?

It's stuck.
Er sitzt fest.
air zitst fest.

Can you push me?
Können Sie mich schieben?
KERN'en zee mikh SHEE-ben?

---

1. Pronounce *ü* like "ee" with your lips in a tight circle.
2. *kh* is a guttural sound.
3. Stress the syllables in capital letters.

Thank you very much.
Vielen Dank.
FEEL-en dahnk.

You are very kind.
Sie sind sehr liebenswürdig.
zee zint zair LEE-bens-vür-dikh.

I want to speak to the mechanic.
Ich möchte den Mechaniker sprechen.
ikh MERKH-teh den meh-KHA-nik-er SHPREKH'en.

He doesn't work on weekends.
Er arbeitet nicht am Wochenende.
air AH-by-tet nikht ahm VO-khen-end-eh.

The car doesn't go well.
Der Wagen läuft nicht gut.
dair VA-ghen loyft nikht goot.

What's the matter?
Was ist los?
vahss isst lohss?

The motor makes a funny noise.
Der Motor macht ein eigenartiges Geräusch.
*dair MO-tor mahkht ine EYE-ghen-art-ig-ess
    gheh-ROYSH.*

It's difficult to start.
Er ist schwierig zu starten.
air isst SHVEE-rikh ts'oo SHTART'en.

Can you fix it?
Können Sie es reparieren?
KERN'en zee ess ray-pa-REER'en?

What will it cost?
Was wird es kosten?
vahss veert ess KO-sten?

How long will it take?
Wie lange wird es dauern?
vee LAHNG-eh veert ess DOW-ern?

Today it isn't possible.
Heute ist es nicht möglich.
HOY-teh isst ess nikht MERG-likh.

Perhaps tomorrow.
Vielleicht morgen.
feel-LY'KHT MOR-ghen.

When will it be ready?
Wann wird es fertig sein?
vahn veert ess FER-tikh zyne?

In two hours.
In zwei Stunden.
in ts'vy SHTOON-den.

To make sure exactly when the car will be ready, consult the phrases in the "Time" section, page 32.

Point to the Answer

Zeigen Sie bitte auf dieser Seite Ihre Antwort auf meine Frage. Danke.
Please point on this page to your answer to my question. Thank you.

Das wird Sie —— Mark kosten.
It will cost you —— marks.

Es wird in —— Stunden fertig sein.
It will be ready in —— hours.

Es wird in —— Tagen fertig sein.
It will be ready in —— days.

---

1. Pronounce *ü* like "ee" with your lips in a tight circle.
2. *kh* is a guttural sound.
3. Stress the syllables in capital letters.

Morgen.
Tomorrow.

Übermorgen.
The day after tomorrow.

Wir haben nicht den Bestandteil.
We don't have the part.

Wir können das vorübergehend reparieren.
We can repair it temporarily.

International Road Signs

Danger

Main road ahead

Caution

Sharp turn

Right curve

Left curve

Crossroads

One way

Do not enter

Guarded RR crossing

Unguarded RR crossing

No parking

Parking

Bumps

---

1. Pronounce *ü* like "ee" with your lips in a tight circle.
2. *kh* is a guttural sound.
3. Stress the syllables in capital letters.

In addition, you will see or hear the following instructions:

RECHTS FAHREN
rekhts FAR'en
Keep to the right

UMLEITUNG
OOM-lye-toong
Detour

EINBAHNSTRASSE
INE-bahn-shtrahss-eh
One way

KREUZUNG
KROY-ts'oong
Crossroads

HÖCHSTGESCHWINDIGKEIT 100 KM.
HERKST-ghe-shvin-dikh-kite HOON-dert
   KEEL-oh-mait-er
Maximum speed 100 kilometers per hour

PARKEN VERBOTEN
PARK'en fair-BO-ten
No parking

AUTOBAHN EINFAHRT
OW-toh-bahn INE-fahrt
Autobahn entrance

AUSFAHRT
OWSS-fahrt
Exit

GESPERRT
gheh-SHPAIRT
Road closed

✤ 12. Sightseeing and Photography

We have combined these two important sections, since you will want to take pictures of what you are seeing. If you are taking pictures indoors, be sure to ask the custodian **Ist es erlaubt?**—"Is it permitted?"

Sightseeing

I need a guide.
Ich brauche einen Reiseführer.
ikh BROW-kheh INE-en RYE-zeh-für-er.

Are you a guide?
Sind Sie ein Reiseführer?
zint zee ine RYE-zeh-für-er?

Do you speak English?
Sprechen Sie Englisch?
SHPREKH'en zee EHNG-lish?

It doesn't matter.
Es macht nichts.
ess mahkht nikhts.

I speak a little German.
Ich spreche ein wenig Deutsch.
ikh SHPREKH-eh ine VAY-nikh doytch.

Do you have a car?
Haben Sie einen Wagen?
HAHB'en zee INE-en VA-ghen?

---

1. Pronounce *ü* like "ee" with your lips in a tight circle.
2. *kh* is a guttural sound.
3. Stress the syllables in capital letters.

What do you charge per hour?
Was kostet es pro Stunde?
vahss KO-stet ess pro SHTOON-deh?

How much per day?
Wieviel pro Tag?
vee-FEEL pro tahk?

For two people.
Für zwei Personen.
für ts'vy pair ZOHN-en.

A group of four.
Eine Gruppe von vier.
INE-eh GROOP-eh fohn feer.

We want to see the old part of the city.
Wir möchten die Altstadt sehen.
veer MERKHT'en dee AHLT-shtaht ZAY'en.

Where is the railroad terminal?
Wo ist der Bahnhof?
vo isst dair BAHN-hohf?

We want to go . . .   . . . to the museum.
Wir wollen . . .   . . . ins Museum gehen.
veer VOHL'en . . .   . . . ins moo-ZAY-oom GAY'en.

. . . to the park.
. . . in den Park gehen.
. . . in den park GAY'en.

. . . to the Town Hall.
. . . zum Rathaus gehen.
. . . ts'oom RAHT-howss GAY'en.

. . . to the zoo.   **. . . to the market.**
. . . zum Zoo gehen.   . . . zum Markt gehen.
. . . ts'oom ts'oh GAY'en.   *. . . ts'oom markt GAY'en.*

. . . to the Hofbrau.
. . . zum Hofbräuhaus gehen.
. . . *ts'oom HOHF-broy-howss GAY'en.*

Observe that gehen—"to go"—comes at the end of the phrase, not at the beginning, as in English. When two verbs are used together, the second one, which is in the form of an infinitive or a participle, regularly comes at the end.

We want to take a trip around the city.
Wir möchten eine Stadtrundfahrt machen.
veer MERKH-ten INE-eh STAHT-roont-fahrt MAKH'en.

How beautiful!
Wie schön!
vee shern!

Very interesting!
Sehr interessant!
zair in-teh-reh-SAHNT!

From what period is this?
Aus welcher Zeit stammt dies?
owss VEL-kher ts'ite shtahmt deess?

Do you know a good cabaret?
Kennen Sie ein gutes Kabarett?
KEN'en zee ine GOOT-es ka-ba-RAY?

Let's go!
Gehen wir!
GAY'en veer!

You are a very good guide.
Sie sind ein guter Führer.
zee zint ine GOOT-er FÜR-er.

Come again tomorrow.
Kommen Sie morgen wieder.
KOHM'en zee MOR-ghen VEE-der.

At nine o'clock.
Um neun Uhr.
oom noyn oor.

---

1. Pronounce *ü* like "ee" with your lips in a tight circle.
2. *kh* is a guttural sound.
3. Stress the syllables in capital letters.

And, if you don't have a guide:

May one enter?
Darf man eintreten?
darf mahn INE-trayt'en?

It is open. Es ist geöffnet. *ess isst ghe-ERF-net.*	**It is closed.** Es ist geschlossen. *ess isst ghe-SHLOSS'en.*

It opens at two o'clock.
Es wird um zwei Uhr geöffnet.
ess veert oom ts'vy oor ghe-ERF-net.

What are the visiting hours?
Wann sind die Besuchszeiten?
vahn zint dee beh-ZOOKHS-ts'y-ten?

It is closed for repairs.
Wegen Reparaturarbeiten geschlossen.
VAY-ghen reh-pa-ra-TOOR-ar-bite'en ghe-SHLOSS'en.

Can one take photos?
Darf man photographieren?
darf mahn fo-toh-grahf-EER'en?

It is permitted. Es ist erlaubt. *ess isst air-L'OWPT.*	**It is forbidden.** Es ist verboten. *ess isst fair-BO-ten.*

Leave your packages in the checkroom.
Lassen Sie ihr Gepäck in der Garderobe.
LAHSS'en zee eer ghe-PAYK in dair gar-deh-RO-beh.

Leave your camera here.
Lassen Sie Ihre Kamera hier.
LAHSS'en zee EER-eh KA-meh-ra heer.

What is the admission?
Was kostet der Eintritt?
vahss KO-stet dair INE-trit?

One mark.
Eine Mark.
INE-eh mark.

And for children?
Und für Kinder?
oont für KIN-der?

The admission is free.
Der Eintritt ist frei.
dair INE-trit isst fry.

Your ticket, please!
Ihre Eintrittskarte, bitte!
EER-eh INE-trits-kar-teh, BIT-teh!

Follow me!
Folgen Sie mir!
FOLG'en zee meer!

No smoking.
Rauchen verboten.
R'OWKH'en fair-BO-ten.

This way please!
Hierher, bitte!
HEER-hair, BIT-teh!

This castle . . .
Diese Burg . . .
DEE-zeh boork . . .

This palace . . .
Dieses Schloß . . .
DEE-zehss shloss . . .

This church . . .
Diese Kirche . . .
DEE-zeh KEER-kheh . . .

This monument . . .
Dieses Denkmal . . .
*DEE-zehss
    DEHNK-mahl . . .*

This street . . .
Diese Straße . . .
DEE-zeh SHTRAHSS-eh . . .

This square . . .
Dieser Platz . . .
DEE-zer plahtz . . .

---

1. Pronounce *ü* like "ee" with your lips in a tight circle.
2. *kh* is a guttural sound.
3. Stress the syllables in capital letters.

... is very interesting.	It's magnificent!
... ist sehr interessant.	Es ist großartig!
... isst zair in-teh-reh-SAHNT.	*ess isst GROSS-art-ikh!*

It's very old, isn't it?	This is for you.
Es ist sehr alt, nicht wahr?	Das ist für Sie.
ess isst zair ahlt, nikht vahr?	*dahss isst für zee.*

Some signs you may see in public places:

HERREN *or* MÄNNER	DAMEN *or* FRAUEN
HAIR-en *MEN-er*	*DA-men* *FROW-en*
Gentlemen Men	Ladies Women

EINGANG	AUSGANG	DRÜCKEN	ZIEHEN
INE-gahng	*OWSS-gahng*	*DRÜK'en*	*TS'EE'en*
Entrance	Exit	Push	Pull

AUF	ZU	KALT	WARM	HEISS
owf	*ts'oo*	*kahlt*	*vahrm*	*hice*
On	Off	Cold	Warm	Hot

BESUCHSZEITEN	AUSKUNFT
beh-ZOOKHS-ts'y-ten	*OWSS-koonft*
Visiting hours	Information

ZUTRITT VERBOTEN	GARDEROBE
TS'OO-trit fair-BO-ten	*gar-deh-RO-beh*
No admission	Checkroom

RAUCHEN VERBOTEN
R'OW-khen fair-BO-ten
No smoking

Verboten on signs has the general connotation of "No!" or "Don't do it!"; so when you see it, don't walk on the grass, smoke, take pictures, or whatever the case may be.

Photography

Where is a camera shop?
Wo ist ein Fotogeschäft?
vo isst ine FO-toh-ghe-sheft?

I need some film for my camera.
Ich brauche etwas Film für meinen Foto-Apparat.
*ikh BROW-khe ET-vahss film für MY-nen
   FO-toh-ah-pa-RAHT.*

. . . black and white.   **. . . color film.**
. . . schwarz-weiß.   . . . Farbfilm.
. . . shvarts-vice.   *. . . FARP-film.*

. . . movie film.
. . . Film für Film-Kamera.
. . . Film für FILM-ka-meh-ra.

This is to be developed.
Das muß entwickelt werden.
dahss mooss ent-VIK-elt VAIRD'en.

How much per print?   **Two prints of each.**
Was kostet ein Abzug?   Von jedem Bild zwei.
vahss KO-stet ine AHP-ts'ook? *fon YAID-em bilt ts'vy.*

An enlargement.
Eine Vergrößerung.
INE-eh fair-GRER-seh-roong.

---

1. Pronounce *ü* like "ee" with your lips in a tight circle.
2. *kh* is a guttural sound.
3. Stress the syllables in capital letters.

About this size.
Ungefähr diese Größe.
oon-ghe-FAIR DEE-zeh GRER-seh.

When will it be ready?
Wann wird es fertig sein?
vahn veert ess FAIR-tikh zine?

Flash bulbs.
Blitzlichtbirnen.
BLITZ-likht-beer-nen.

For this camera.
Für diese Kamera.
für DEE-zeh KA-meh-ra.

May I take a photograph of you?
Darf ich Sie photographieren?
dahrf ikh zee fo-toh-gra-FEER'en?

Stand here, please.
Stellen Sie sich hierher, bitte.
SHTEL'en zee zikh HEER-hair, BIT-teh.

Don't move!
Nicht bewegen!
nikht beh-VAYG'en!

Smile!
Lächeln!
LAIKH'eln!

That's it.
Das wär's.
dahss vairss.

Will you please take one of me?
Würden Sie bitte eine von mir machen?
VURD'en zee BIT-teh INE-eh fohn meer MAKH'en?

In front of this.
Davor.
da-FOR.

You are very kind.
Sie sind sehr freundlich.
zee zint zair FROYND-likh.

May I send you a copy?
Darf Ich Ihnen einen Abzug senden?
darf ikh EE-nen INE-en AHP-ts'ook ZEN-den?

Your name, please?
Ihr Name, bitte?
eer NA-meh, BIT-teh?

Your address?
Ihre Adresse?
EER-eh ah-DRESS-eh?

Point to the Answer

Zeigen Sie bitte auf dieser Seite Ihre Antwort auf meine Frage. Danke.
Please point on this page to your answer to my question. Thank you.

Kommen Sie morgen zurück.	**Um ———— Uhr.**
Come back tomorrow.	At ———— o'clock.

Kommen Sie in ———— Tagen zurück.
Come back in ———— days.

Wir können es reparieren.	**Wir können es nicht re-**
We can repair it.	**parieren.**
	We cannot repair it.

Wir haben keines.
We don't have any.

Asking to take pictures of someone often leads to more general conversation. For this reason the following three sections will be especially interesting to you.

🦅 13. Entertainment

Things to Do

May I invite you . . .
Darf ich Sie . . .
dahrf ikh zee . . .

. . . to lunch?
. . . zum Mittagessen einladen?
. . . ts'oom MIT-tahk-ess-en INE-lahd'en?

. . . to dinner?
. . . zum Abendessen einladen?
. . . ts'oom AH-bent-ess-en INE-lahd'en?

. . . for a drink?
. . . zu einem Getränk einladen?
. . . ts'oo INE-em ghe-TRENK INE-lahd'en?

. . . for a drive?
. . . zu einer Fahrt einladen?
. . . ts'oo INE-er fahrt INE-lahd'en?

. . . to play bridge?
. . . zum Bridge einladen?
. . . ts'oom bridge INE-lahd'en?

. . . to the movies?
. . . ins Kino einladen?
. . . ins KEE-no INE-lahd'en?

. . . to the theater?
. . . ins Theater einladen?
. . . ins teh-AH-ter INE-lahd'en?

... to play golf?	... to play tennis?
... zum Golf einladen?	... zum Tennis einladen?
... ts'oom gohlf INE-lahd'en?	... ts'oom TEN-nis INE-lahd'en?

Einladen—"to invite"—comes at the end of each sentence, in accordance with German word order.

May I ask you to dance?
Darf ich Sie um den Tanz bitten?
dahrf ikh zee oom den tahn'ts BIT'en?

Thank you very much!	**With pleasure!**
Vielen Dank!	Mit Vergnügen!
FEEL-en dahnk!	*mit fairg-NÜ-ghen!*

I am sorry.	**I cannot.**
Es tut mir leid.	Ich kann nicht.
ess toot meer lite.	*ikh kahn nikht.*

I am busy.	**I am tired.**
Ich bin beschäftigt.	Ich bin müde.
ikh bin beh-SHEFT-eekht.	*ikh bin MÜ-deh.*

I am waiting for someone.
Ich warte auf jemanden.
ikh VAR-teh owf YEH-mahn-den.

I don't feel well.
Ich fühle mich nicht gut.
ikh FÜ-leh mikh nikht goot.

Let's go ...	**... to the beach.**
Gehen wir ...	... an den Strand.
GAY'en veer ...	*... ahn den shtrahnt.*

---

1. Pronounce *ü* like "ee" with your lips in a tight circle.
2. *kh* is a guttural sound.
3. Stress the syllables in capital letters.

. . . to the meeting.
. . . zur Konferenz.
. . . *ts'oor kohn-fair-ENTZ.*

. . . to a nightclub.
. . . ins Nachtlokal.
. . . *inss NAHKHT-lo-kahl.*

. . . to a small restaurant.
. . . in eine Gaststätte.
. . . *in INE-eh GAHST-shtet-eh.*

. . . to a beer hall.
. . . in eine Bierhalle.
. . . *in INE-eh BEER-hahl-leh.*

. . . to the movies.
. . . ins Kino.
. . . *inss KEE-no.*

. . . to a beer garden.
. . . in einen Biergarten.
. . . *in INE-en BEER-gar-ten.*

Where are we going tomorrow?
Wohin gehen wir morgen?
vo-HIN GAY'en veer MOR-ghen?

Let's go . . .	. . . to see the town.
Gehen wir . . .	. . . die Stadt anschauen.
GAY'en veer . . .	. . . *dee shtaht AHN-sh'ow'en.*

. . . to an art show.
. . . zu einer Kunstausstellung.
. . . *ts'oo INE-er KOONST-owss-shtel-loong.*

. . . to the opera.
. . . in die Oper.
. . . *in dee OH-per.*

... to the art museum.
... zum Kunstmuseum.
... *ts'oom KOONST-moo-zay-oom.*

... to the market place.   **... to the cathedral.**
... zum Marktplatz.   ... zum Dom.
... *ts'oom MARKT-plahtz.*   ... *ts'oom dohm.*

... to the old Town Hall.
... zum alten Rathaus.
... *ts'oom AHL-ten RAHT-howss.*

... to the harbor.   **... to the park.**
... zum Hafen.   ... zum Park.
... *ts'oom HA-fen.*   ... *ts'oom park.*

... to the zoo.
... zum Zoo.
... *ts'oom ts'oh.*

... to the observation tower.
... zum Aussichtsturm.
... *ts'oom OWSS-zikhts-toorm.*

... to the football game.
... zum Fußballspiel.
... *ts'oom FOOS-bahl-shpeel.*

... to the horse races.
... zum Pferderennen.
... *ts'oom PFAIR-deh-ren'en.*

Who is ahead?
Wer gewinnt?
vair geh-VINT?

---

1. Pronounce *ü* like "ee" with your lips in a tight circle.
2. *kh* is a guttural sound.
3. Stress the syllables in capital letters.

Theaters and Nightclubs

Let's go to the theater.
Gehen wir ins Theater.
GAY'en veer inss teh-AH-ter.

Two seats, please!
Zwei Plätze, bitte!
ts'vy PLET-seh, BIT-teh!

Orchestra.
Parkett.
par-KET.

Balcony.
Balkon.
bahl-KOHN.

Are they good seats?
Sind es gute Plätze?
sint ess GOO-teh PLET-seh?

When does it start?
Wann fängt es an?
vahn fengt ess ahn?

Reserve two seats for me, please.
Reservieren Sie, bitte, zwei Plätze für mich.
reh-zehr-VEE-ren zee, BIT-teh, ts'vy PLET-seh für mikh.

Who is playing the lead?
Wer spielt die Hauptrolle?
vair shpeelt dee HOWPT-roll-eh?

She is beautiful.
Sie ist schön.
zee isst shern.

How do you like it?
Wie gefällt es Ihnen?
vee geh-FELT ess EEN-en?

Very good!
Sehr gut!
zair goot!

It's great!
Es ist großartig!
ess isst GROSS-ar-tikh!

It's very amusing.
Es ist sehr amüsant.
ess isst zair ah-mŭ-ZAHNT.

Is it already over?
Schon zu Ende?
shohn ts'oo EN-deh?

And now let's go dance.
Und jetzt gehen wir tanzen.
oont yetzt GAY'en veer TAHN-ts'en.

A table near the dance floor, please.
Einen Tisch nahe der Tanzdiele, bitte.
INE-en tish NA-eh der TAHNTS-dee-leh, BIT-eh.

Shall we dance?
Wollen wir tanzen?
VOL'en veer TAHNTS'en?

Shall we stay a little while?
Wollen wir noch bleiben?
VOHL'en veer nohkh BLY-ben?

Shall we go?
Wollen wir gehen?
VOHL'en veer GAY'en?

---

1. Pronounce *ŭ* like "ee" with your lips in a tight circle.
2. *kh* is a guttural sound.
3. Stress the syllables in capital letters.

Invitations to Dinner

Can you come for dinner at our house?
Können Sie zum Abendessen zu uns kommen?
KERN'en zee ts'oom AH-bent-ess-en ts'oo oons KOHM'en?

. . . Monday at eight?
. . . Montag, um acht?
. . . *MOHN-tahk, oom akht?*

With great pleasure!
Mit großem Vergnügen!
mit GROSS-em fairg-NÜG-en!

If it isn't inconvenient for you.
Wenn es Ihnen nicht ungelegen ist.
ven ess EE-nen nikht OON-ghe-leh-ghen isst.

Sorry I am late.
Es tut mir leid, daß ich spät komme.
ess toot meer lite, dahss ikh shpayt KO-meh.

The traffic was awful.
Der Verkehr war entsetzlich.
der fair-KAIR vahr ent-ZETS-likh.

Very happy to see you.
Sehr erfreut, Sie wiederzusehen.
zair air-FROYT zee VEE-der-ts'oo-zay'en.

Make yourself at home!
Fühlen Sie sich wie zu Hause!
FÜ-len zee zikh vee ts'oo HOW-zeh!

What a beautiful house!
Was für ein schönes Haus!
vahss fur ine SHERN-ess howss!

Will you have something to drink?
Möchten Sie etwas zu trinken?
MERK-ten zee ET-vahss ts'oo TRINK'en?

A cigarette?
Eine Zigarette?
INE-eh ts'ig-ah-RET-teh?

To your health!
Auf Ihr Wohl!
owf eer vōhl!

Dinner is served!
Das Abendessen ist serviert!
dahss AH-bent-ess-en isst sair-VEERT!

Will you sit here?
Wollen Sie hier sitzen?
VOHL-len zee heer ZITS'en?

What a delicious meal!
Was für ein köstliches
Essen!
*vahss für ine KERST-likh-
ess ESS'en!*

It tastes great!
Es schmeckt großartig!
ess shmekt GROSS-art-ikh!

Do have some more!
Nehmen Sie doch mehr!
NAY-men zee dokh mair!

We had a wonderful time!
Wir hatten viel Vergnügen!
veer HAHT'en feel fairg-NÜG-en!

We enjoyed visiting you.
Es war sehr nett bei Ihnen.
ess vahr zair nett by EEN-en.

---

1. Pronounce *ü* like "ee" with your lips in a tight circle.
2. *kh* is a guttural sound.
3. Stress the syllables in capital letters.

We must go!
Wir müssen gehen!
veer MÜSS'en GAY'en!

That is a pity!
Wie schade!
vee SHA-deh!

I'll take you home.
Ich bringe Sie nach Hause.
ikh BRING-eh zee nahkh HOW-zeh.

No, please don't bother!
Nein, bitte bemühen Sie sich nicht!
nine, BIT-teh beh-MÜ'en zee sikh nikht!

Many thanks for your hospitality!
Vielen Dank für Ihre Gastfreundschaft!
FEEL-en dahnk für EER-eh GAHST-froynt-shahft!

See you again soon!
Auf baldiges Wiedersehen!
owf BAHL-tee-ghess VEE-der-zay'en!

🦅 14. Talking to People

Most phrase books are too preoccupied with attending to one's wants and generally "getting along" to pay much attention to what you should say once you have met someone. The following expressions have been tested for everyday conversational frequency and use and, except for the rather special phrases at the end of the section, will be of immediate use for making conversation with anyone you meet.

Do you live in this city?
Wohnen Sie in dieser Stadt?
VO-nen zee in DEE-zer shtaht?

Where are you from?
Wo kommen Sie her?
vo KOHM'en zee hair?

I am from Munich.
Ich komme aus München.
ikh KOHM-eh owss MÜNT-yen.

Really?	**It's a beautiful city!**
Wirklich?	Es ist eine schöne Stadt!
VEERK-likh?	*ess isst INE-eh SHERN-eh shtaht!*

I've been there.	**I would like to go there.**
Ich war dort.	Ich möchte dorthin fahren.
ikh var dort.	*ikh MERKH-teh DORT-hin FAR'en.*

How long have you been here?
Wie lange sind Sie schon hier?
vee LAHNG-eh zint zee shohn heer?

1. Pronounce *ü* like "ee" with your lips in a tight circle.
2. *kh* is a guttural sound.
3. Stress the syllables in capital letters.

Three days.
Drei Tage.
dry TAHG-eh.

Several weeks.
Einige Wochen.
EYE-nig-eh VOKH-en.

Two months.
Zwei Monate.
ts'vy MO-na-teh.

How long will you stay here?
Wie lange werden Sie hier bleiben?
vee LAHNG-eh VAIRD'en zee heer BLY-ben?

I will stay for one month.
Ich werde einen Monat bleiben.
ikh VAIRD-eh INE-en MO-naht BLY-ben.

Have you been here before?
Waren Sie schon früher hier?
VAR'en zee shohn FRÜ-er heer?

Yes, once.
Ja, einmal.
ya, INE-mahl.

Five years ago.
Vor fünf Jahren.
for fünf YA-ren.

A long time ago.
Vor langer Zeit.
for LAHNG-er ts'ite.

Before the war.
Vor dem Krieg.
for dem kreek.

Where are you living?
Wo wohnen Sie?
vo VOHN'en zee?

At what hotel?
In welchem Hotel?
in VEL-khem ho-TEL?

How do you like Vienna?
Wie gefällt Ihnen Wien?
vee ghe-FAILT EEN-en veen?

I like it very much.
Ich mag es sehr.
ikh mahk ess zair.

Very interesting.
Sehr interessant.
Zair in-teh-reh-SAHNT.

The women are very beautiful.
Die Frauen sind sehr schön.
dee FROW-en zint zair shern.

Do you come from the United States?
Kommen Sie von den Vereinigten Staaten?
KOHM'en vee fohn den fair-EYE-nikh-ten SHTAHT-en?

Yes, from San Francisco.
Ja, von San Franzisko.
ya, fohn San Francisco.

I speak a little German.
Ich spreche ein wenig Deutsch.
ikh SHPREKH-eh ine VEH-nikh doych.

Your pronunciation is good.
Ihre Aussprache ist gut.
EER-eh OWSS-shpra-kheh isst goot.

You are very kind.
Sie sind sehr liebenswürdig.
zee zint zair LEE-bens-vûr-dikh.

Have you been in the United States?
Waren Sie schon in den Vereinigten Staaten?
VAR'en zee shohn in den fair-EYE-nikh-ten SHTAHT-en?

. . . in England?	**Where did you go?**
. . . in England?	Wo waren Sie?
. . . in EHNG-lahnt?	*vo VAR'en zee?*

What do you think of . . . ?
Was halten Sie von . . . ?
vahss HAHLT'en zee fohn . . . ?

---

1. Pronounce *û* like "ee" with your lips in a tight circle.
2. *kh* is a guttural sound.
3. Stress the syllables in capital letters.

. . . **American movies?**
. . . amerikanischen Filmen?
. . . *ah-meh-ree-KA-nee-shen FILM-en?*

. . . **German music?**
. . . deutscher Musik?
. . . *DOY-cher moo-ZEEK?*

. . . **German books?**
. . . deutschen Büchern?
. . . *DOY-chen BÜ-khern?*

When people ask your opinion about something, you will find the following comments most helpful.

Very interesting.
Sehr interessant.
zair in-teh-reh-SAHNT.

Great!
Großartig!
GROSS-art-ikh!

Magnificent!
Prachtvoll!
PRAKHT-fohl!

Marvelous!
Wunderbar!
VOON-der-bar!

Not bad.
Nicht schlecht.
nikht shlekht.

Sometimes.
Manchmal.
MAHNKH-mahl.

Once.
Einst.
ine'st.

Never.
Niemals.
NEE-mahlss.

Often.
Oft.
ohft.

It seems to me that . . .
Es scheint mir, daß . . .
ess shine't meer, dahss . . .

In any case . . .
Auf jeden Fall . . .
owf YEH-den fahl . . .

Really?
Wirklich?
VEERK-likh?

That's too bad!
Das ist schade!
dahss isst SHA-deh!

I don't know.
Ich weiß nicht.
ikh vice nikht.

I have forgotten.
Ich habe vergessen.
ikh HAHB-eh fair-GUESS'en.

I agree with you.
Ich bin Ihrer Meinung.
ikh bin EER-er MY-noong.

Of course.
Selbstverständlich.
zelpst-fair-SHTEND-likh.

Is it possible?
Ist es möglich?
isst ess MERG-likh?

Unbelievable!
Unglaublich!
oon-GL'OWB-likh!

You must come to see us soon.
Sie müsen uns bald besuchen.
zee MÜSS'en oons bahlt beh-ZOOKH'en.

At our house.
Bei uns zu Hause.
by oons ts'oo HOW-zeh.

With pleasure.
Mit Vergnügen.
mit fairg-NÜG-en.

Are you married?
Sind Sie verheiratet?
zint zee fair-HI-raht-et?

I am married.
Ich bin verheiratet.
ikh bin fair-HI-raht-et.

I am not married.
Ich bin nicht verheiratet.
ikh bin nikht fair-HI-raht-et.

---

1. Pronounce *ü* like "ee" with your lips in a tight circle.
2. *kh* is a guttural sound.
3. Stress the syllables in capital letters.

Do you have children?
Haben Sie Kinder?
HAHB'en zee KIN-der?

No, I haven't.
Nein, ich habe keine.
nine, ikh HAHB-eh KYE-neh.

Yes, I have children.
Ja, ich habe Kinder.
yah, ikh HAHB-eh KIN-der.

How many girls?
Wieviel Mädchen?
VEE-feel MAID-khen?

How many boys?
Wieviel Jungen?
VEE-feel YOONG'en?

How old are they?
Wie alt sind sie?
vee ahlt zint zee?

My son is seven years old.
Mein Sohn ist sieben Jahre alt.
mine zohn isst ZEE-ben YA-reh ahlt.

My daughter is ten years old.
Meine Tochter ist zehn Jahre alt.
MY-neh TOKH-ter isst ts'ayn YA-reh ahlt.

What cute children!
Was für süße Kinder!
vahss für ZÜ-seh KIN-der!

This is my . . .
Das ist meine . . .
*dahss isst
   MY-neh . . .*

. . . mother.
. . . Mutter.
. . . MOOT-er.

. . . wife.
. . . Frau.
. . . frow.

. . . sister.
. . . Schwester.
. . . SHVESS-ter.

. . . daughter.
. . . Tochter.
. . . TOKH-ter.

. . . daughter-in-law.
. . . Schwiegertochter.
. . . SHVEE-gher-tokh-ter.

. . . granddaughter.
. . . Enkelin.
. . . EN-kel-in.

This is my . . .   . . . father.   . . . husband.
Das ist mein . . .   . . . Vater.   . . . Mann.
dahss isst   *. . . FA-ter.*   *. . . mahn.*
  mine . . .

. . . brother.   . . . son.   . . . grandson.
. . . Bruder.   . . . Sohn.   . . . Enkel.
. . . BROOD-er.   *. . . zohn.*   *. . . ENK-el.*

. . . son-in-law.   . . . Do you know
. . . Schwiegersohn.   . . . Kennen Sie
. . . SHVEE-gher-zohn.   *. . . KEN-nen zee*

. . . Mr. Peters?   . . . that man?
. . . Herrn Peters?   . . . diesen Mann?
. . . Hairn PAY-terss?   *. . . DEE-zen mahn?*

. . . Mrs. Muller?   . . . that lady?
. . . Frau Müller?   . . . diese Dame?
. . . frow MÜL-er?   *. . . DEE-zeh DA-meh?*

He is . . .   . . . a writer.
Er ist . . .   . . . Schriftsteller.
air isst . . .   *. . . SHRIFT-shtel-ler.*

. . . an artist.   . . . a businessman.
. . . Künstler.   . . . Geschäftsmann.
. . . KÜNST-ler.   *. . . ghe-SHEFTS-mahn.*

. . . a lawyer.   . . . a doctor.
. . . Rechtsanwalt.   . . . Arzt.
. . . REKHTS-ahn-vahlt.   *. . . arts't.*

---

1. Pronounce *ü* like "ee" with your lips in a tight circle.
2. *kh* is a guttural sound.
3. Stress the syllables in capital letters.

... a manufacturer.
... Fabrikant.
... *fa-bree-KAHNT.*

... a banker.
... Bankier.
... *bahnk-YEH.*

... an actor.
... Schauspieler.
... *SH'OW-shpeel-er.*

... my husband.
... mein Mann.
... *mine mahn.*

... a soldier.
... Soldat.
... *zohl-DAHT.*

She is ...
Sie ist ...
zee isst ...

... an airline hostess.
... Stewardesse.
... *STEW-ar-dess-eh.*

... a writer. (f)
... Schriftstellerin.
... *SHRIFT-shtel-ler-in.*

... an artist. (f)
... Künstlerin.
... *KÜNST-ler-in.*

... a painter.
... Maler.
... *MA-ler.*

... a professor.
... Professor.
... *pro-FESS-or.*

... a member of the
government.
... Regierungsmitglied.
... *reh-GEER-oongs-
mit-gleet.*

... an officer.
... Offizier.
... *oh-fee-TS'EER.*

... an actress.
... Schauspielerin.
... *SH'OW-shpeel-er-in.*

... teacher. (f)
... Lehrerin.
... *LAIR-er-in.*

... a doctor. (f)
... Ärztin.
... *AIRTS-tin.*

... my wife.
... meine Frau.
... *MY-neh frow.*

He is an American.	**She is an American.**
Er ist Amerikaner.	Sie ist Amerikanerin.
air isst ah-meh-ree-	*zee isst ah-meh-ree-*
KAHN-er.	*KAHN-er-in.*
He is a German.	**She is a German.**
Er ist Deutscher.	Sie ist Deutsche.
air isst DOYCH-er.	*zee isst DOYCH-eh.*
He is an Austrian.	**She is an Austrian.**
Er ist Österreicher.	Sie ist Österreicherin.
air isst ER-stair-RYE-kher.	*zee isst ER-stair-*
	RYE-kher-in.
He is a Swiss.	**She is a Swiss.**
Er ist Schweizer.	Sie ist Schweizerin.
air isst SHVITE-ser.	*zee isst SHVITE-ser-in.*
He is an Englishman.	**She is an English woman.**
Er ist Engländer.	Sie ist Engländerin.
air isst EHNG-len-der.	*zee isst EHNG-len-der-in.*
He is a Canadian.	**She is a Canadian.**
Er ist Kanadier.	Sie ist Kanadierin.
air isst ka-NAHD-yer.	*zee isst ka-NAHD-yer-in.*

See dictionary for other selected nationalities.

He (she) is very intelligent.
Er (Sie) ist sehr intelligent.
air (zee) isst zair in-tel-lee-GHENT.

He (she) is very nice.
Er (Sie) ist sehr nett.
air (zee) isst zair net.

---

1. Pronounce *ü* like "ee" with your lips in a tight circle.
2. *kh* is a guttural sound.
3. Stress the syllables in capital letters.

He (she) is very capable.
Er (Sie) ist sehr tüchtig.
air (zee) isst zair tükh-tikh.

This is my address.
Das ist meine Adresse.
dahss isst MINE-eh ah-DRESS-eh.

What is your (his, her) address?
Was ist Ihre (seine, ihre) Adresse?
vahss isst EER-eh (ZY-neh, EER-eh) ah-DRESS-eh?

Here is my telephone number.
Hier ist meine Telefonnummer.
heer isst MINE-eh teh-leh-FOHN-noom-er.

What is your telephone number?
Wie ist Ihre Telefonnummer?
vee isst EER-eh teh-leh-FOHN-noom-er?

May I call you?
Darf ich Sie anrufen?
darf ikh zee AHN-roof'en?

When?
Wann?
vahn?

Tomorrow morning.
Morgen Vormittag.
MOR-ghen FOR-mit-tahk.

Early.
Früh.
frü.

In the afternoon.
Am Nachmittag.
ahm NAKH-mit-tahk.

What is your first name?
Wie ist Ihr Vorname?
vee isst eer FOR-na-meh?

My first name is Peter.
Mein Vorname ist Peter.
mine FOR-na-meh isst PAY-ter.

You dance very well.
Sie tanzen sehr gut.
zee TAHN-ts'en zair goot.

You sing very well.
Sie singen sehr gut.
zee ZING'en zair goot.

I like your dress.
Mir gefällt Ihr Kleid.
meer ghe-FALT eer klite.

I have a surprise for you.
Ich habe eine Überraschung für Sie.
ikh HAHB-eh INE-eh über-RAHSH-oong für zee.

Do you like it?
Gefällt es Ihnen?
ghe-FELT ess EEN-en?

May I see you again?
Darf ich Sie wiedersehen?
darf ikh zee VEE-der-zay'en?

When?
Wann?
vahn?

Where?
Wo?
vo?

What's the matter?
Was ist los?
vahss isst lohss?

Are you angry?
Sind Sie böse?
zint zee BER-zeh?

Why?
Warum?
va-ROOM?

Where are you going?
Wo gehen Sie hin?
vo GAY'en zee hin?

Let's go together!
Gehen wir zusammen!
GAY'en veer ts'oo-ZAHM-en!

---

1. Pronounce *ü* like "ee" with your lips in a tight circle.
2. *kh* is a guttural sound.
3. Stress the syllables in capital letters.

You are very clever.
Sie sind sehr klug.
zee zint zair klook.

You are very pretty . . .
Sie sind sehr hübsch . . .
zee zint zair hübsch . . .

and very charming too.
und auch sehr sympathisch.
*oont owkh zair
    seem-PA-tish.*

You are very nice.
Sie sind sehr nett.
zee zint zair net.

I like you very much.
Ich mag Sie sehr gern.
ikh mahk zee zair gairn.

What do you think of me?
Was halten Sie von mir?
vahss HAHLT'en zee fohn meer?

I love you.
Ich liebe dich.
ikh LEEB-eh dikh.

Are you serious?
Meinst du es ernst?
MINE'st doo ess airnst?

Will you give me your photograph?
Wirst du mir dein Foto geben?
veerst doo meer dine FO-toh GAY-ben?

Will you write to me?
Wirst du mir schreiben?
veerst doo meer SHRY-ben?

Don't forget!
Nicht vergessen!
nikht fair-GUESS'en!

In the last five sentences we have used the familiar form for "you," both in the verb and the pronoun, since the tone of the conversation implies a certain degree of familiarity. See the introduction to the "Dictionary" for more about the familiar form.

🦅 15. Words That Show You Are "With It"

There are certain words that German-speaking people use constantly but that do not always have an exact equivalent in English. To use them at the right time will cause German people to consider that you have not only a diploma in good manners but also an excellent foundation in German culture patterns—in other words, that you are "with it." The German expressions are given first to make it easier for you to recognize them as they occur in everyday conversation.

We have divided these terms into two groups. The first is composed of selected polite expressions:

Verzeihung!
fair-TS'Y-oong!
Pardon me!

Gute Reise!
GOOT-eh RYE-zeh!
Have a good trip!

Herzlich willkommen!
HAIRTS-likh vil-KOHM-en!
A hearty welcome!

Prosit!
PRO-zit!
Here's to you!

Guten Appetit!
GOOT-en ahp-peh-TEET!
Enjoy your meal!

Auf Ihre Gesundheit!
owf EER-eh ghe-ZOONT-hitz!
To your good health!

---

1. Pronounce *ü* like "ee" with your lips in a tight circle.
2. *kh* is a guttural sound.
3. Stress the syllables in capital letters.

Alles Gute!	**Viel Glück!**
AH-less GOOT-eh!	*feel glük!*
All the best! (or)	Good luck!
Have a good time!	

Hals und Beinbruch!
hahlss oont BINE-brookh!
Good luck! (literally "Neck and leg break!")

Herzliche Glückwünsche!	**Mein Beileid!**
HAIRTS-likh-eh	*mine BY-lite!*
GLÜK-vün-sheh!	My sympathy!
Congratulations!	

Mit besten Grüßen!	**Gute Besserung!**
mit BESS-ten GRÜ-sen!	*GOOT-eh BESS-eh-roong!*
With best regards!	Get well!

Viele Grüsse an ———!
FEEL-eh GRÜSS-eh ahn ———!
My regards to ———!

As the following phrases permeate conversation, it will interest you to know what they mean, as well as to learn to use them as useful conversational stopgaps. The translations are extremely free, as these expressions are very idiomatic.

Nicht wahr?	**Doch**
nikht var?	*dohkh*
Isn't it? (or) Don't you think so?	then (or) however

Jawohl!	**Es tut mir leid!**	**Dann**
ya-VOHL!	*ess toot meer lite!*	*dahnn*
Yes, indeed!	I'm sorry!	then

Wie, bitte?
vee, BIT-teh?
How's that?

Bitte sehr.
BIT-teh zair.
Please (or) You're welcome.

Gehen wir!
GAY'en veer!
Let's go!

Das ist schrecklich!
dahss isst SHREK-likh!
That's terrible!

Das macht nichts.
dahss makht nikhts.
It doesn't matter.

Das ist mir egal.
dahss isst meer eh-GAHL.
I don't care.

Prima!
PREE-ma!
The best!

Großartig!
GROSS-art-ikh!
Wonderful!

Einverstanden!
INE-fer-shtahnd'en!
O.K.

Abgemacht!
AHP-ghe-mahkht!
It's a deal!

Natürlich.
na-TÜR-likh.
Naturally.

Irgendwo.
EER-ghent-vo.
Somewhere.

Irgendwie.
EER-ghent-vee.
Somehow.

Selbstverständlich.
zelbst-fair-SHTEND-likh.
Of course.

Aber nein!
AH-bair nine!
But no!

Aber ja!
AH-bair ya!
But yes!

Ebenfalls!
AIB-en-fahlss!
Mutually (or)
Same to you!

---

1. Pronounce *ü* like "ee" with your lips in a tight circle.
2. *kh* is a guttural sound.
3. Stress the syllables in capital letters.

Bestimmt.
beh-SHTIMMT.
Definitely.

Wirklich?
VEERK-likh?
Really?

Tatsächlich.
taht-ZEKH-likh.
Indeed.

Sofort!
zo-FORT!
Right away!

Hören Sie mal!
her'en zee mahl!
Listen! (or) Look here!

Was Sie nicht sagen!
vahss zee nikht ZA-ghen!
You don't say!

Gar nicht.
gar nikht.
Not at all.

Übrigens.
Ü-bree-ghenss.
Incidentally.

Um Gottes Willen!
oom GOHT-ess VILL-en!
For God's sake! (or) For Heaven's sake!

Mein Gott!
mine goht!
My God (or) Good heavens!

Gott sei Dank!
goht zye dahnk!
Thank God! (or)
Thank goodness!

 # 16. Shopping

Shops in Germany, Austria, and Switzerland still tend to be specialized, although there exist chains of general stores and even the supermarket—**Supermarkt**.

Some additional shop signs you will see include **Delikatessen**, which should need no translation but means a specialty food shop, and **Drogerie**, which does not exactly correspond to "drugstore" as it sells only soap, perfumes, and cosmetics. **Boutique** is frequently used for small shops. On some cafés or small shops **bei** (at the house of) precedes a proper name. **Bei Giesele** means "at Giesele's house" or "at Giesele's."

Names of Shops

Is there a . . . around here?
Gibt es in der Nähe . . .
ghipt ess in dair NAY-eh . . .

. . . a department store?
. . . ein Warenhaus?
. . . *ine VAR-en-howss?*

. . . a dress shop?
. . . ein Kleidergeschäft?
. . . *ine KLY-der-ghe-sheft?*

. . . a hat shop?
. . . ein Hutgeschäft?
. . . *ine HOOT-ghe-sheft?*

. . . a shoe store?
. . . ein Schuhgeschäft?
. . . *ine SHOO-ghe-sheft?*

. . . a jewelry shop?
. . . ein Juweliergeschäft?
. . . *ine yoo-veh-LEER-ghe-sheft?*

. . . a drugstore? (for soap, cosmetics, perfumes, etc.)
. . . eine Drogerie?
. . . *INE-eh dro-ghe-REE?*

---

1. Pronounce *ü* like "ee" with your lips in a tight circle.
2. *kh* is a guttural sound.
3. Stress the syllables in capital letters.

... **a pharmacy?** (for medicines)
... eine Apotheke?
... *INE-eh ah-po-TEH-keh?*

... **a bookshop?**
... eine Buchhandlung?
... *INE-eh BOOKH-hahnt-loong?*

... **a toy shop?**
... ein Spielzeuggeschäft?
... *ine SHPEEL-ts'oyk-ghe-sheft?*

... **a flower shop?**
... einen Blumenladen?
... *INE-en BLOOM-en-la-den?*

... **an antique shop?**
... ein Antiquitätengeschäft?
... *ine ahn-tee-kvee-TAYT-en-geh-sheft?*

... **a grocery store?**
... einen Kolonialwarenladen?
... *INE-en ko-lohn-YAHL-va-ren-la-den?*

... **a market?**   ... **a camera shop?**
... einen Markt?   ... ein Fotogeschäft?
... *INE-en markt?*   ... *ine FO-toh-ghe-sheft?*

... **a tobacco shop?**   ... **a barber shop?**
... einen Tabakladen?   ... einen Friseur?
... *INE-en ta-BAHK-la-den?*   ... *INE-en free-ZER?*

... **a beauty parlor?**
... einen Damenfriseur?
... *INE-en DA-men-free-ZER?*

General Shopping Vocabulary

BARGAIN SALE
AUSVERKAUF
OWSS-fer-kowf

May I help you?	**What do you wish?**
Darf ich Ihnen helfen?	Was wünschen Sie?
darf ikh EEN-en HELL-fen?	*vahss VÜN-shen zee?*

I would like something . . .
Ich möchte etwas . . .
ikh MERKH-teh ET-vahss . . .

. . . for my husband.	**. . . for my wife.**
. . . für meinen Mann.	. . . für meine Frau.
. . . für MY-nen mahn.	*. . . für MY-neh frow.*

. . . for a man.	**. . . for a lady.**
. . . für einen Herren.	. . . für eine Dame.
. . . für INE-en hairn.	*. . . für INE-eh DA-meh.*

Do you need something?	**At the moment—nothing.**
Brauchen Sie etwas?	Momentan—nichts.
BROW-khen zee ET-vahss?	*mo-men-TAHN nikhts.*

I'm just looking around.
Ich sehe mir bloß alles an.
ikh ZAY-eh meer blohss AH-less ahn.

I'll be back later.
Ich komme später wieder.
ikh KOHM-eh SHPAY-ter VEE-der.

---

1. Pronounce *ü* like "ee" with your lips in a tight circle.
2. *kh* is a guttural sound.
3. Stress the syllables in capital letters.

I like this.   ... that.   How much is it?
Ich mag dies.   ... das.   Wieviel macht es?
ikh mahk deess.   *... dahss.*   *vee-FEEL makht ess?*

Show me another.
Zeigen Sie mir ein anderes.
TS'Y-ghen zee meer ine AHN-der-ess.

Something not so expensive.   Do you like this?
Etwas nicht so teuer.   Gefällt das Ihnen?
ET-vahss nikht zo TOY-er.   *geh-FELT dahss EEN-en?*

May I try it on?
Darf ich es anprobieren?
darf ikh ess AHN-pro-beer'en?

That suits you marvelously!
Das paßt Ihnen wunderbar!
dahss pahst EEN-en VOON-der bar!

Good, I'll take it.
Gut, ich nehme es.
goot, ikh NEH-meh ess.

Can you alter it?
Können Sie es umändern?
KERN-en zee ess OOM-end-ern?

Is it handmade?   Is it hand embroidered?
Ist es Handarbeit?   Ist es handgestickt?
isst ess HAHNT-ar-bite?   *isst ess HAHNT-ghe-shtikt?*

Would you wrap it?
Würden Sie es einpacken?
VÜR-den zee ess INE-pahk'en?

Can I pay by check?
Kann ich mit einem Scheck zahlen?
kahn ikh mit INE-em shek TS'AHL'en?

Can you send it to this address?
Können Sie es an diese Adresse senden?
KERN'en zee ess ahn DEE-zeh ah-DRESS-eh ZEND'en?

A receipt, please.
Eine Quittung, bitte.
INE-eh KVIT-toong, BIT-teh.

The change, please.
Das Wechselgeld, bitte.
*dahss VEX-el-ghelt,
   BIT-teh.*

And some small change.
Und etwas Kleingeld.
*oont ET-vahss
   KLINE-ghelt.*

Come back again!
Kommen Sie bald wieder!
KOHM'en zee bahlt VEE-der!

ON SALE
ZUM VERKAUF
ts'oom fair-KOWF

Point to the Answer

Zeigen Sie bitte auf dieser Seite Ihre Antwort auf meine
   Frage. Danke.
Please point on this page to your answer to my question.
   Thank you.

Wir haben keines.
We haven't any.

Das ist alles, was wir haben.
That's all we have.

Wir haben nichts größeres.
We haven't anything larger.

Wir haben nichts kleineres.
We haven't anything
   smaller.

Wir liefern nicht.
We don't deliver.

---

1. Pronounce *ü* like "ee" with your lips in a tight circle.
2. *kh* is a guttural sound.
3. Stress the syllables in capital letters.

Wir können es an eine Adresse in Amerika senden.
We can send it to an address in America.

Was ist Ihre Adresse?
What is your address?

Wir können nicht persönliche Schecks nehmen.
We cannot accept personal checks.

Wir nehmen Reiseschecks.
We accept traveler's checks.

Clothes

a blouse	a suit	a coat
eine Bluse	ein Anzug	ein Mantel
INE-eh BLOO-zeh	*ine AHN-ts'ook*	*ine MAHN-tel*

a hat	a scarf	a handbag
ein Hut	ein Schal	eine Handtasche
ine hoot	*ine shahl*	*INE-eh HAHNT-ta-sheh*

gloves	shoes	stockings
Handschuhe	Schuhe	Strümpfe
HAHNT-shoo-eh	*SHOO-eh*	*STRÜMPF-eh*

a slip	a brassiere
ein Unterrock	ein Büstenhalter
ine OONT-er-rohk	*ine BÜ-sten-hahl-ter*

panties	a nightgown
Schlüpfer	ein Nachthemd
SHLÜP-fer	*ine NAKHT-hemt*

a bathrobe	slippers
ein Bademantel	Pantoffeln
ine BA-deh-mahn-tel	*pahn-TOHF-feln*

an evening dress
ein Abendkleid
ine AH-bent-klite

a raincoat
ein Regenmantel
ine REH-ghen-mahn-tel

boots
Stiefel
SHTEE-fel

an umbrella
ein Regenschirm
ine REH-ghen-sheerm

a swimsuit
ein Badeanzug
ine BA-deh-ahn-ts'ook

sandals
Sandalen
zahn-DAHL-en

a skirt
ein Rock
ine rohk

pants
Hosen
HO-zen

a jacket
eine Jacke
INE-eh YA-keh

a tie
eine Krawatte
INE-eh kra-VAHT-teh

socks
Socken
ZOHK-en

an overcoat
ein Mantel
ine MAHN-tel

undershorts
Unterhosen
OONT-er-ho-zen

an undershirt
ein Unterhemd
ine OONT-er-hemt

pajamas
Pyjama
pee-JAHM-ah

handkerchiefs
Taschentücher
TAHSH-en-tükh-er

Sizes—Colors—Materials

What size?
Welche Größe?
VELL-kheh GRER-seh?

---

1. Pronounce *ü* like "ee" with your lips in a tight circle.
2. *kh* is a guttural sound.
3. Stress the syllables in capital letters.

small	medium	large	larger
klein	mittel	groß	größer
kline	*MIT-el*	*gross*	*GRER-ser*

smaller	wider	narrower	longer
kleiner	weiter	enger	länger
KLINE-er	*VITE-er*	*EHNG-er*	*LENG-er*

shorter	What color?
kürzer	Welche Farbe?
KÜR-ts'er	*VEL-kheh FAR-beh?*

blue	red	yellow	green	lilac
blau	rot	gelb	grün	lila
bl'ow	*roht*	*ghelp*	*grün*	*LEE-la*

brown	gray	black	white
braun	grau	schwarz	weiß
brown	*gr'ow*	*shvarts*	*vice*

darker	lighter
dunkler	heller
DOONK-ler	*HELL-er*

Is it silk?	wool	linen
Ist es Seide?	Wolle	Leinen
isst ess ZY-deh?	*VOHL-leh*	*LYE-nen*

nylon	dacron	leather	suede
Nylon	Dacron	Leder	Wildleder
NEE-lohn	*DAHK-rohn*	*LAY-der*	*VILD-lay-der*

kid	cotton	plastic
Ziegenleder	Baumwolle	Kunststoff
TS'EE-ghen-lay-der	*B'OWM-vohl-leh*	*KOONST-stohff*

fur	What kind of fur?	fox	beaver
Pelz	Was für ein Pelz?	Fuchs	Biber
pelts	*vahss für ine pelts?*	*fooks*	*BEE-ber*

seal	mink	leopard	rabbit
Seehund	Nerz	Leopard	Kaninchen
ZAY-hoont	*nairts*	*leh'o-PART*	*kah-NEEN-khen*

Newsstand

I would like to have . . .
Ich möchte haben . . .
ikh MERKH-teh HAHB'en . . .

a guidebook
· einen Reiseführer
INE-en RYE-zeh-für-er

a map of the city
einen Stadtplan
INE-en STAHT-plahn

sunglasses
eine Sonnenbrille
INE-eh ZOHN-nen-bril-eh

postcards
Postkarten
POST-kar-ten

some paper
etwas Papier
ET-vahss pa-PEER

this magazine
diese Zeitschrift
DEE-zeh TS'ITE-shrift

an American newspaper
eine amerikanische Zeitung
INE-eh ah-meh-ree-KA-nee-sheh TS'ITE-oong

Tobacco Shop

Have you American cigarettes?
Haben Sie amerikanische Zigaretten?
HAHB'en zee ah-meh-ree-KA-nee-sheh ts'ee-ga-RET-en?

---

1. Pronounce *ü* like "ee" with your lips in a tight circle.
2. *kh* is a guttural sound.
3. Stress the syllables in capital letters.

a pipe
eine Pfeife
INE-eh PFY-feh

tobacco
Tabak
ta-BAHCK

cigars
Zigarren
ts'ee-GA-ren

matches
Streichhölzer
SHTRY'KH-herl-ts'er

a lighter
ein Feuerzeug
ine FOY-er-ts'oyk

lighter fluid
Benzin
ben-TS'EEN

Drugstore

a toothbrush
eine Zahnbürste
INE-eh TS'AHN-bůr-steh

toothpaste
Zahnpasta
TS'AHN-pa-sta

a razor
ein Rasierapparat
ine ra-ZEER-ah-par-raht

razor blades
Rasierklingen
ra-ZEER-kling-en

shaving cream
Rasiercreme
ra-ZEER-krehm

a hairbrush
eine Haarbürste
INE-eh HAR-bůr-steh

a comb
ein Kamm
ine kahm

aspirin
Aspirin
ah-spear-EEN

iodine
Jod
yoht

scissors
eine Schere
INE-eh SHAIR-eh

a nailfile
eine Nagelfeile
INE-eh NA-ghel-fy-leh

anitseptic
antiseptisches Mittel
ahn-tee-SEP-tish-es MIT-el

cough medicine
Hustensaft
HOOSS-ten-zahft

cough drops
Hustenbonbons
HOOSS-ten-bohn-bohnss

Cosmetics

powder
Puder
POO-der

lipstick
Lippenstift
LIP-pen-shtift

nail polish
Nagellack
NA-ghel-lahk

mascara
Wimperntusche
VIM-pern-too-sheh

cleansing cream
Reinigungscreme
*RYE-nee-goongs-
kreh-meh*

shampoo
Schampo
shahm-POO

eyebrow pencil
Augenbraustift
*OW-ghen-brow-
shtift*

bobby pins
Haarklammern
HAR-klahm-ern

hair pins
Haarnadeln
HAR-nahd-eln

hairspray
Haarlack
HAR-lahk

perfume
Parfum
par-FAHM

That smells good, doesn't it?
Das riecht gut, nicht wahr?
dahss reekht goot, nikht var?

Hairdresser

Wash and set, please.
Waschen und Legen, bitte.
VA-shen oont LAY-ghen, BIT-teh.

Not so hot!
Nicht so heiß!
nikht zo hicel

a manicure
eine Maniküre
*INE-eh ma-nee-
KÜ-reh*

lighter
heller
HELL-er

darker
dunkler
DOONK-ler

---

1. Pronounce *ü* like "ee" with your lips in a tight circle.
2. *kh* is a guttural sound.
3. Stress the syllables in capital letters.

Barber

a shave	a haircut	a massage
rasieren	ein Haarschnitt	eine Massage
ra-ZEE'ren	*ine HAR-shnit*	*INE-eh ma-SA-zheh*

Use scissors!	shorter	not too short
Mit der Schere!	kürzer	nicht zu kurz
mitt dair SHEH-reh!	*KUR-ts'er*	*nikht ts'oo koorts*

on top	in back	the sides	That's fine!
oben	hinten	die Seiten	Das ist gut!
OH-ben	*HIN-ten*	*dee ZY-ten*	*dahss isst goot!*

Food Market

I would like . . .	. . . a dozen . . .
Ich möchte . . .	. . . ein Dutzend . . .
ikh MERKH-teh . . .	*. . . ine DOOTS-ent*

. . . of these.	. . . of those.
. . . von diesen.	. . . von denen.
. . . fohn DEE-zen.	*. . . fohn DEH-nen.*

I want five.	Is this fresh?
Ich möchte fünf.	Ist das frisch?
ikh MERKH-teh fünf.	*isst dahss frish?*

Three cans of these preserves.
Drei Büchsen dieser Konserven.
dry BÜKH-zen DEE-zer kohn-ZAIR-ven.

How much per kilo?
Wieviel das Kilo?
vee-FEEL dahss KEE-lo?

Weight is measured by the kilo (kilogram—**kilogramm**) rather than by the pound. One kilo is equivalent to 2.2 pounds.

Do you have wine here?
Gibt es Wein hier?
ghipt ess vine heer?

What is this?
Was ist das?
vahss isst dahss?

strong liquor
Schnaps
shnahps

In a bag, please!
In eine Tüte, bitte!
in INE-eh TÜ-teh, BIT-teh!

Jewelry

I would like to buy . . .
Ich möchte kaufen . . .
ikh MERKH-teh KOW-fen . . .

a watch
eine Uhr
INE-eh oor

a ring
einen Ring
INE-en ring

a necklace
ein Halsband
ine HAHLSS-bahnt

a bracelet
ein Armband
ine ARM-bahnt

earrings
Ohrringe
OHR-ring-eh

Is it gold?
Ist es aus Gold?
isst ess owss gohlt?

silver
Silber
ZIL-ber

platinum
Platin
pla-TEEN

---

1. Pronounce *ü* like "ee" with your lips in a tight circle.
2. *kh* is a guttural sound.
3. Stress the syllables in capital letters.

Is it silver-plated?
Ist es versilbert?
isst ess fair-ZEEL-bairt?

Is it gold-plated?
Ist es vergoldet?
isst ess fair-GOHL-det?

a diamond
ein Diamant
ine dee-ah-MAHNT

a ruby
ein Rubin
ine ROO-bin

pearls
Perlen
PAIR-len

a sapphire
ein Saphir
ine zah-FEER

Antiques

What period is this?
Aus welcher Zeit stammt dies?
owss VEL-kher ts'ite shtahmt deess?

It's beautiful!
Es ist schön!
ess isst shern!

But very expensive.
Aber sehr teuer.
AH-ber zair TOY-er.

How much is . . .
Was kostet . . .
vahss KO-stet . . .

. . . this book?
. . . dieses Buch?
. . . DEE-zes bookh?

. . . this picture?
. . . dieses Bild?
. . . DEE-zess BILT?

. . . this frame?
. . . dieser Rahmen?
. . . DEE-zer RA-men?

. . . this map?
. . . diese Landkarte?
. . . DEE-zeh LAHNT-kar-teh?

. . . this piece of furniture?
. . . dieses Möbelstück?
. . . DEE-zess MER-bel-shtük?

Can you have it sent?
Können Sie es schicken lassen?
KERN'en zee ess SHICK'en LAHSS'en?

... to this address?
... an diese Adresse?
... ahn DEE-zeh ah-DRESS-eh?

---

1. Pronounce *ü* like "ee" with your lips in a tight circle.
2. *kh* is a guttural sound.
3. Stress the syllables in capital letters.

17. Telephone

Talking on the phone is an excellent test of your ability to communicate in German because you can't see the person you are talking to nor use gestures to get your meaning across. When asking for someone, simply say his name and add bitte. If you say the number instead of dialing, say the numbers in pairs: 79–65–83 would be neunundsiebzig–fünfundsechzig–dreiundachtzig.

Where is the telephone?
Wo ist das Telefon?
vo isst dahss teh-leh-FOHN?

The telephone operator.	Hello.
Das Telefonfräulein.	Hallo.
dahss teh-leh-FOHN-froy-line.	*HA-lo.*

Please, the telephone number of ———.
Bitte, die Telefonnummer von ———.
BIT-teh, dee teh-leh-FOHN-noom-er fohn ———.

Connect me, please, with number ——— in Berlin.
Verbinden Sie mich, bitte, mit der Nummer ——— in Berlin.
fair-BIN-den zee mikh, BIT-teh, mit dair NOOM-er ——— in bair-LEEN.

Information.	Long distance.
Auskunft.	Ferngespräch.
OWSS-koonft.	*fairn-ghe-SHPREKH.*

I am calling number ———, extension 339.
Ich rufe Nummer ———, Apparat drei–drei–neun.
ikh ROO-feh NOOM-er ———, ahp-pa-RAHT dry–dry–noyn.

How long must I wait?
Wie lange muß ich warten?
vee LAHNG-eh moos ikh VART'en?

How much is it per minute?
Wieviel kostet es pro Minute?
vee-FEEL KO-stet ess pro mee-NOO-teh?

My number is ———.
Meine Nummer ist ———.
MINE-eh NOOM-er isst ———.

Mr. Schmidt, please.
Herrn Schmidt, bitte.
hairn shmit, BIT-teh.

He (she) isn't here.
Er (Sie) ist nicht da.
air (zee) isst nikht da.

Please say it once more.
Bitte sagen Sie es noch
einmal.
*BIT-teh ZAHG'en zee ess
nokh ine-MAHL.*

Hold the line!
Bleiben Sie am Apparat!
*BLYB'en zee ahm
ahp-pa-RAHT!*

One moment!
Einen Augenblick!
INE-en OW-ghen-blik!

When is he (she) coming back?
Wann kommt er (sie) zurück?
vahn kohmt air (zee) ts'oo-RÜK?

Thank you, I'll call back.
Danke schön, ich rufe wieder an.
DAHN-keh shern, ikh ROOF-eh VEE-der ahn.

Can you give him (her) the following message?
Können Sie ihm (ihr) das Folgende mitteilen?
*KERN'en zee eem (eer) dahss FOHL-ghen-deh
MIT-tile'en?*

---

1. Pronounce *ü* like "ee" with your lips in a tight circle.
2. *kh* is a guttural sound.
3. Stress the syllables in capital letters.

Please ask him (her) to call me.
Bitten Sie ihn (sie) mich anzurufen.
BIT'en zee een (zee) mikh AHN-ts'oo-roof'en.

I'll give you my number.
Ich gebe Ihnen meine Nummer.
ikh GAY-beh EEN-en MINE-eh NOOM-er.

This is Brown speaking.
Hier spricht Brown.
heer shprikt brown.

I'll spell it: B—R—O—W—N.
Ich buchstabiere: B—R—O—W—N.
ikh bookh-shta-BEER-eh: bay-air-o-vay-en.

A	B	C	D	E	F
ah	*bay*	*ts'ay*	*day*	*eh*	*ef*

G	H	I	J	K	L
gay	*ha*	*ee*	*yoht*	*kah*	*el*

M	N	O	P	Q	R
em	*en*	*oh*	*pay*	*koo*	*air*

S	T	U	V	W	X
ess	*tay*	*oo*	*fow*	*vay*	*ix*

Y	Z
IP-see-lohn	*ts'et*

Although some American and English names are fairly easy to say in German, others are often strange to German ears. You will find the spelled-out alphabet very useful for spelling your name when you leave a message.

Where can I make a phone call here?
Wo kann ich hier telefonieren?
vo kahn ikh heer teh-leh-fohn-EER'en?

Where is a pay phone?
Wo gibt es einen Zahlfernsprecher?
vo ghipt ess INE-en TS'AHL-fairn-shprekh-er?

the telephone book
das Telefonbuch
dahss teh-leh-FOHN-bookh

What kind of coin do I put in?
Was für ein Geldstück muß ich hineintun?
vahss für ine GHELT-shtük moos ikh hin-INE-toon?

Can you change one mark into 10-pfennig pieces for me?
Können Sie mir eine Mark in Zehnpfennigstücke wechseln?
*KERN'en zee meer INE-eh mark in
 TS'AYN-pfen-nikh-shtük-eh VEX-eln?*

And if there is no public telephone available:

May I use your phone?
Dürfte ich Ihr Telefon benutzen?
DÜRF-teh ikh eer teh-leh-FOHN beh-NOOTS'en?

Certainly.
Natürlich.
na-TÜR-likh.

How much do I owe you?
Was schulde ich Ihnen?
*vahss SHOOL-deh ikh
 EEN-en?*

Hello, Operator.
Hallo Zentrale.
HA-lo ts'en-TRA-leh.

I got a wrong number.
Ich war falsch verbunden.
*ikh var fahlsh
 fair-BOOND'en.*

---

1. Pronounce *ü* like "ee" with your lips in a tight circle.
2. *kh* is a guttural sound.
3. Stress the syllables in capital letters.

✦18. Post Office and Telegrams

One of the first things one does when abroad is to write postcards—**Postkarten**—to friends and relatives. Here is how to mail them. You might also impress your friends by adding a few words in German, which you will find at the end of this section.

Where is the post office?
Wo ist das Postamt?
vo isst dahss POST-amht?

. . . a mailbox?
. . . ein Briefkasten?
. . . ine BREEF-kahst-en?

Five ten-pfennig stamps.
Fünf Zehnpfennigmarken.
fünf TS'AYN-p'fen-nikh-MARK-en.

How much is needed?
Wieviel braucht man?
vee-FEEL browkht mahn?

Air-mail.
Per Luftpost.
pair LOOFT-post.

For a letter to the United States.
Für einen Brief in die Vereinigten Staaten.
für INE-en breef in dee fair-INE-nikh-ten SHTAHT-en.

For a letter to Canada.
Für einen Brief nach
Kanada.
*für INE-en breef nakh
KA-na-da.*

. . . to Spain.
. . . nach Spanien.
. . . nakh SHPA-nee-en.

. . . to Holland.
. . . nach Holland.
. . . nakh HOHL-lahnt.

. . . to Russia.
. . . nach Russland.
. . . nakh ROOS-lahnt.

. . . to England.
. . . nach England.
. . . nakh EHNG-lahnt.

. . . to France.
. . . nach Frankreich.
. . . nakh FRAHNK-rye'kh.

... to Switzerland.   ... to Austria.
... in die Schweiz.   ... nach Österreich.
... in dee shvy'ts.·   *... nakh ER-stair-rye'kh.*

For the names of other selected countries, see the dictionary.

Registered.   **Insured.**
Eingeschrieben.   Versichert.
INE-ghe-shree-ben.   *Fair-ZICH-ert.*

Where can I send a telegram?
Wo kann ich ein Telegram abschicken?
Vo kahn ikh ine teh-leh-GRAHM AHP-schick'en?

How much does each syllable cost?
Was kostet die Silbe?
vahss KO-stet dee ZEEL-beh?

I need writing paper.   **Envelopes.**
Ich brauche Schreibpapier.   Briefumschläge.
ikh BROW-khe SHRIBE-   *BREEF-oom-shleh-gheh.*
pa-PEER.

Can you lend me a pen?
Können Sie mir einen Kugelschreiber leihen?
KERN'en zee meer ine-en KOO-gel-shry-ber LY'en?

Can you lend me a pencil?
Können Sie mir einen Bleistift leihen?
KERN'en zee meer INE-en BLY-shtift LY'en?

Can you give me some stamps?
Können Sie mir einige Briefmarken geben?
KERN'en zee meer INE-ig-eh BREEF-mark-en GAYB'en?

---

1. Pronounce *ü* like "ee" with your lips in a tight circle.
2. *kh* is a guttural sound.
3. Stress the syllables in capital letters.

Dear John,   **Dear Jane,**
Lieber Hans,   Liebe Johanna,
LEE-ber Hahnss,   *LEE-beh yo-HA-na,*

All best regards from Munich.
Viele Grüße aus München.
FEE-leh GRÜS-seh owss MÜNT-yen.

I miss you very much.
Sie fehlen mir sehr.
zee FAIL'en meer zair.

Best wishes to everyone.
Die besten Wünsche an alle.
dee BESS-ten VÜN-sheh ahn AHL-eh.

Sincerely,   **With love!**
Herzlichst,   Allerherzlichst!
HAIRTS-likhst,   *AHL-er-HAIRTS-likhst!*

Yours, (m)   **Yours,** (f)   **Yours,** (pl)
Ihr,   Ihre,   *Ihre,*
eer   *EER-eh*   *EER-eh*

🦅 19. Seasons and Weather

winter	spring	summer	autumn
Winter	Frühling	Sommer	Herbst
VIN-ter	*FRÜ-ling*	*ZO-mer*	*Hairpst*

How is the weather?
Wie ist das Wetter?
vee isst dahss VET-ter?

The weather is fine.
Das Wetter ist schön.
dahss VET-ter isst shern.

It is very hot.
Es ist sehr heiß.
ess isst zair hice.

It is cold.
Es ist kalt.
ess isst kahlt.

It is raining.
Es regnet.
ess RAYG-net.

It is 20° (68°F) today.
Es ist 20 Grad heute.
ess isst TS'VAHN-ts'ikh grahd HOY-teh.

Temperature is expressed in centigrade, not Fahrenheit. Zero is freezing in centigrade, and 100° is boiling. To change centigrade to Fahrenheit, multiply by 9/5 and add 32°; to change Fahrenheit to centigrade, subtract 32° and multiply by 5/9.

Let's go swimming!
Gehen wir schwimmen!
GAY'en veer SHVIM'en!

Where is the pool?
Wo ist das Schwimmbad?
vo isst dahss SHVIM-baht?

I need an umbrella.
Ich brauche einen Regenschirm.
Ikh BROW-kheh INE-en RAY-ghen-sheerm.

---

1. Pronounce *ü* like "ee" with your lips in a tight circle.
2. *kh* is a guttural sound.
3. Stress the syllables in capital letters.

... a raincoat.
... einen Regenmantel.
... *INE'en RAY-ghen-mahn-tel.*

... boots.
... Stiefel.
... *SHTEE-fel.*

What a fog!
Was für ein Nebel!
vahss für ine NEH-bel!

One can't see a thing.
Man kann nichts sehen.
mahn kahn nikhts ZAY-en.

It's snowing.
Es schneit.
ess shnite.

Do you like to ski?
Laufen Sie gerne Schi?
LOWF'en zee GAIR-neh shee?

... to ice-skate?
... Schlittschuh?
... *SHLEET-shoo?*

I want to rent skis.
Ich möchte Schier mieten.
ikh MERKH-teh SHEE-er MEET'en.

I want to rent ice skates.
Ich möchte Schlittschuhe mieten.
ikh MERKH-teh SHLEET-shoo-eh MEET'en.

🦅 20. Doctor and Dentist

Doctor

I am ill.
Ich bin krank.
ikh bin krahnk.

My wife ..
Meine Frau ...
MY-neh frow ...

My husband ...
Mein Mann ...
mine mahn ...

My daughter...
Meine Tochter ...
MY-neh TOKH-ter ...

My son ...
Mein Sohn ...
mine zohn ...

My friend ...
Mein Freund...
mine froynt ...

... is ill.
... ist krank.
... isst krahnk.

I don't feel well.
Ich fühle mich nicht wohl.
ikh FÜL-eh mikh nikht vohl.

We need a doctor.
Wir brauchen einen Arzt.
veer BROW-kh'en INE-en artst.

When can he come?
Wann kann er kommen?
vahn kahn air KOHM'en?

Well, what's wrong with you?
Nun, was ist los mit Ihnen?
noon, vahss isst lohss mit EEN-en?

Where does it hurt?
Wo tut es weh?
vo toot ess vay?

Here.
Hier.
heer.

I have a pain ..
Ich habe Schmerzen ...
ikh HAHB-eh SHMAIR-ts'en ...

... in the head.
... im Kopf.
... im kohpf.

---

1. Pronounce *ü* like "ee" with your lips in a tight circle.
2. *kh* is a guttural sound.
3. Stress the syllables in capital letters.

He (she) has a pain . . .
Er (Sie) hat Schmerzen . . .
air (zee) haht SHMAIR-ts'en . . .

. . . in the throat.
. . . im Hals.
. . . im hahlss.

. . . in the ear.
. . . im Ohr.
. . . im ohr.

. . . in the stomach
. . . im Bauch.
. . . im bowkh.

. . . in the foot.
. . . im Fuß.
. . . im foos.

. . . in the back.
. . . im Rücken.
. . . im RÜ-ken.

. . . in the leg.
. . . im Bein.
. . . im bine.

. . . in the arm.
. . . im Arm.
. . . im arm.

. . . in the hand.
. . . in der Hand.
. . . in dair hahnt.

I am dizzy.
Mir ist schwindlig.
meer isst SHVIND-likh.

I have a fever.
Ich habe Fieber.
ikh HAHB-eh FEE-ber.

I cannot sleep.
Ich kann nicht schlafen.
ikh kahn nikht SHLAHF'en.

I have diarrhea.
Ich habe Durchfall.
ikh HAHB-eh DOORKH-fahl.

Since when?
Seit wann?
zite vahn?

Since yesterday.
Seit gestern.
zite GUESS-tern.

For two days.
Seit drei Tagen.
zite dry TAHG-en.

What have you eaten?
Was haben sie gegessen?
vahss HAHB'en zee ghe-GUESS'en?

Undress!
Auskleiden!
OWSS-kly-den!

Open your mouth!
Öffnen Sie den Mund!
ERF-nen zee den moont!

Lie down!
Legen Sie sich hin!
LAYG'en zee zikh hin!

Show me your tongue!
Zeigen Sie mir die Zunge!
TS'Y-ghen zee meer dee TS'OONG-eh!

Sit up!
Setzen Sie sich aufrecht!
ZETZ'en zee zikh OWF-rekht!

Cough!
Husten Sie!
HOOST'en zee!

Breathe deeply!
Tief einatmen!
teef INE-aht-men!

Get dressed!
Ziehen Sie sich an!
TS'EE'en zee zikh ahn!

You must stay in bed.
Sie müssen im Bett bleiben.
zee MÜSS'en im bet BLY-ben.

Is it serious?
Ist es schlimm?
isst ess shlim?

You must go to the hospital.
Sie müssen ins Krankenhaus.
zee MÜSS'en inss KRAHNK-en-howss.

Take this prescription.
Nehmen Sie dieses Rezept.
NAYM'en zee DEE-zess reh-TS'EPT.

Take these pills.
Nehmen Sie diese Tabletten.
NAYM'en zee DEE-zeh tahb-LET-ten.

No. It isn't serious.
Nein, es ist nicht schlimm.
nine, ess isst nikht shlimm.

Don't worry.
Machen Sie sich keine Sorgen.
MAHKH'en zee zikh KINE-eh ZOR-ghen.

You have . . .
Sie haben . . .
zee HAHB'en . . .

. . . indigestion.
. . . Verdauungsstörungen.
. . . fair-DOW-oongss-shter-oong-en.

---

1. Pronounce *ü* like "ee" with your lips in a tight circle.
2. *kh* is a guttural sound.
3. Stress the syllables in capital letters.

... an infection.   ... a cold.
... eine Entzündung.   ... eine Erkältung.
... *INE-eh ent-TS'Ün-doong.*   ... *INE-eh air-KEL-toong.*

... appendicitis.
... eine Blinddarmentzündung.
... *INE-eh BLINT-darm-ent-ts'ün-doong.*

... a heart attack.
... einen Herzanfall.
... *INE-en HAIRTS-ahn-fahl.*

Be careful!   **Don't eat too much.**
Seien Sie vorsichtig!   Essen Sie nicht zu viel.
ZYE'en zee FOR-zikh-tikh!   *ESS'en zee nikht ts'oo feel.*

Don't drink any alcohol.
Trinken Sie keinen Alkohol.
TRINK'en zee KINE-en ahl-ko-HOHL.

Except beer, of course.
Außer Bier, natürlich.
OWSS-er beer, na-TÜR-likh.

How do you feel today?
Wie fühlen Sie sich heute?
vee FÜL'en zee zikh HOY-teh?

Badly.   **Better.**   **Much better.**
Schlecht.   Besser.   Viel besser.
Shlekht.   *BES-ser.*   *feel BES-ser.*

The centigrade scale is also used to measure body tem—perature. The normal body temperature is 37 degrees. So if you have anything higher than that, you have a fever —Sie haben Fieber.

Dentist

In the unlikely event that the dentist should hurt you, tell him **Halt, bitte!**—"Stop, please!" or **Einen Augenblick!**—"Wait a moment!" This will give you time to regain your courage.

Can you recommend a dentist to me?
Können Sie mir einen Zahnarzt empfehlen?
KERN'en zee meer INE-en TS'ahn-artst emp-FAIL'en?

I have a toothache.	**It hurts here.**
Ich habe Zahnschmerzen.	Es tut hier weh.
ikh HAHB-eh TS'AHN-shmairts-en.	*ess toot heer vay.*

You need a filling.
Sie haben eine Plombe nötig.
zee HAHB'en INE-eh plohm-beh NER-tikh.

There is an inflammation.
Das ist eine Entzündung.
dahss isst INE-eh ent-TS'ÜN-doong.

I must extract this tooth.
Ich muß diesen Zahn ziehen.
Ikh mooss DEE-zen ts'ahn TS'EE'en.

How long will it take?	**A few minutes.**
Wie lange wird es dauern?	Einige Minuten.
vee LAHNG-eh veert ess DOW-ern?	*EYE-nig-eh mee-NOO-ten.*

An injection against pain, please.
Eine Spritze gegen Schmerzen, bitte.
INE-eh SHPRITS-eh GAY-ghen SHMAIRTS-en, BIT-teh.

---

1. Pronounce *ü* like "ee" with your lips in a tight circle.
2. *kh* is a guttural sound.
3. Stress the syllables in capital letters.

Just fix it temporarily.
Machen Sie es provisorisch.
MAKH'en zee ess pro-vee-ZOHR-ish.

Does it hurt?
Tut es weh?
toot ess vay?

No, not at all.
Nein, überhaupt nicht.
nine, Ü-ber-howpt nikht.

Yes, a little.
Ja, ein bißchen.
ya, ine BISS-yen.

Thank you.
Danke.
DAHN-keh.

Is that all?
Ist das alles?
isst dahss AH-less?

How much do I owe you?
Wieviel bin ich Ihnen schuldig?
vee-FEEL bin ikh EEN-en SHOOL-dikh?

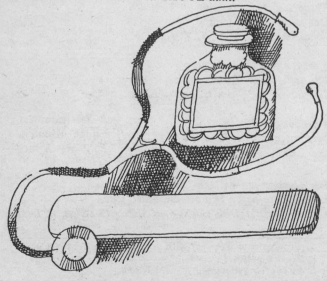

🦅 21. Problems and Police

Although the situations suggested below may never happen to you, the words are useful to know, just in case!

Go away!
Gehen Sie weg!
GAY'en zee vek!

Leave me alone!
Lassen Sie mich allein!
LAHSS'en zee mikh ahl-LINE.

Or I'll call a policeman.
Oder ich rufe die Polizei.
OH-dair ikh ROOF-eh dee po-lee-TS'EYE.

Police!
Polizei!
po-lee-TS'EYE!

Help!
Hilfe!
HEEL-feh!

What's going on?
Was ist los?
vahss isst lohss?

This man is annoying me.
Dieser Mann belästigt mich.
DEE-zair mahn beh-LESS-tikt mikh.

Where is the police station?
Wo ist die Polizeiwache?
vo isst dee po-lee-TS'EYE-vakh-eh?

I have been robbed.
Man hat mich beraubt.
mahn haht mikh beh-R'OWPT.

My watch . . .
Meine Uhr . . .
MINE-eh oor . . .

My wallet . . .
Meine Geldtasche . . .
MINE-eh GHELT-tahsh-eh . . .

My jewelry . . .
Mein Schmuck . . .
mine shmook . . .

---

1. Pronounce *ü* like "ee" with your lips in a tight circle.
2. *kh* is a guttural sound.
3. Stress the syllables in capital letters.

My suitcase . . .	My passport . . .
Mein Handkoffer . . .	Mein Pass . . .
mine HAHNT-kof-fer . . .	*mine pahss . . .*

My car . . .	. . . has been stolen.
Mein Wagen . . .	. . . ist gestohlen worden.
mine VA-ghen . . .	*. . . isst ghe-SHTOHL'en VOR-den.*

Stop!	That's the one!
Halt!	Das ist er!
hahlt!	*dahss isst air!*

Do you wish to make a complaint?
Wollen Sie eine Anklage machen?
VOHL'en zee INE-eh AHN-kla-gheh MAHKH'en?

I am innocent.
Ich bin unschuldig.
ikh bin oon-SHOOL-dikh.

I haven't done anything.
Ich habe nichts getan.
ikh HAHB-eh nikhts ghe-TAHN.

I don't recognize him.
Ich erkenne ihn nicht.
ikh air-KEN-neh een nikht.

I need a lawyer.
Ich brauche einen Anwalt.
ikh BROW-kheh INE-en AHN-vahlt.

Notify the American Consulate.
Benachrichtigen Sie das amerikanische Konsulat.
*beh-NAHKH-rikh-tee-ghen zee dahss ah-meh-ree-KAHN-
ish-eh kohn-soo-LAHT.*

It's nothing.	It's a misunderstanding.
Es ist nichts.	Es ist ein Mißverständnis.
ess isst nikhts.	*ess isst ine MISS-fair-shtend-niss.*

Don't worry!	May I go?
Keine Sorgen!	Darf ich gehen?
kine ZORG-en!	*darf ikh GAY'en?*

🦅 22. Housekeeping

The following chapter will be especially interesting for those who plan to stay longer in Germany, Austria, or Switzerland or have occasion to employ German-speaking baby-sitters or household help, abroad or even at home.

What is your name?
Wie ist Ihr Name?
vee isst eer NA-meh?

Can you cook?
Können Sie kochen?
KERN'en zee KOKH'en?

Where did you work before?
Wo haben Sie vorher gearbeitet?
vo HAHB'en zee FOR-hair ghe-AR-by-tet?

Can you take care of a baby?
Können Sie auf ein Baby aufpassen?
KERN'en zee owf ine BAY-bee OWF-pahs-sen?

We will pay you ——— marks per week.
Wir zahlen Ihren ——— Mark pro Woche.
veer TS'AHL'en EER-en ——— Mark pro VO-khe.

Thursday is your day off.
Donnerstag ist Ihr freier Tag.
DOHN-erss-tahk isst eer FRY-er tahk.

This is your room.
Das ist Ihr Zimmer.
dahss isst eer TS'IM-er.

Please clean . . .
Bitte reinigen Sie . . .
BIT-teh RYE-nee-gen zee . . .

. . . the living room.
. . . das Wohnzimmer.
. . . dahss VOHN-ts'im-er.

. . . the bathroom.
. . . das Badezimmer.
. . . dahss BA-deh-ts'im-er.

. . . the kitchen.
. . . die Küche.
. . . dee KÜKH-eh.

---

1. Pronounce *ü* like "ee" with your lips in a tight circle.
2. *kh* is a guttural sound.
3. Stress the syllables in capital letters.

... the bedroom.
... das Schlafzimmer.
... *dahss SHLAHF- ts'im-er.*

... the dining room.
... das Eßzimmer.
... *dahss ESS-ts'im-er.*

Use the vacuum cleaner.
Nehmen Sie den Staubsauger.
NEH-men zee den SHT'OWB-z'ow-gher.

Iron this!
Bügeln Sie dies!
BÜ-gheln zee deess!

Wash the dishes.
Spülen Sie das Geschirr.
SHPUL'en zee dahss ghe-sheer.

Sweep the floor.
Kehren Sie den Fußboden.
KAIR'en zee den FOOSS-bo-den.

... the broom.
... den Besen.
... *den BAYZ-en.*

Polish the silver.
Putzen Sie das Silber.
POOTS'en zee dahss ZEEL-ber.

Make the beds.
Machen Sie die Betten.
MAKH'en zee dee BET-en.

Change the sheets.
Wechseln Sie die Laken.
VEX-eln zee dee LAHK-en.

Wash this.
Waschen Sie dies.
VA-shen zee deess.

Use bleach.
Benutzen Sie Bleichmittel.
BEH-noots'en zee BLY'KH-mit-tel.

Have you done it already?
Haben Sie es schon gemacht?
HAHB'en zee ess shohn ghe-MAKHT?

Put the meat in the refrigerator.
Legen Sie das Fleisch in den Kühlschrank.
LAYG'en zee dahss fly'sh in den KÜL-shrahnk.

Go to the market.
Gehen Sie zum Markt.
GAY'en zee ts'oom markt.

Here is the list.
Hier ist die Liste.
heer isst dee LEES-teh.

If someone calls, write the name here.
Wenn jemand anruft, schreiben Sie hier den Namen auf.
*ven YEH-mahnt AHN-rooft, SHRY-ben zee heer den
NA-men owf.*

I can be reached at this number.
Ich bin unter dieser Number zu erreichen.
ikh bin OONT-er DEE-zer NOOM-er ts'oo er-RYE-khen.

I'll be back at four o'clock.
Ich bin um vier Uhr wieder zurück.
ikh bin oom feer oor VEE-der ts'oo-RÜK.

Give the child its food at one o'clock.
Geben Sie dem Kind sein Essen um eins.
GAYB'en zee dem kint zine ESS-en oom ine'ts.

Give the child a bath.
Baden Sie das Kind.
BAHD'en zee dahss kint.

Put him to bed at eight o'clock.
Bringen Sie es um acht Uhr ins Bett.
BRING'en zee ess oom akht oor inss bet.

Serve lunch at two o'clock.
Bringen Sie das Mittagessen um zwei Uhr.
BRING'en zee dahss MIT-takh-ess-en oom ts'vy oor.

We are having guests for dinner.
Wir haben Gäste zum Abendessen.
veer HAHB'en GUESS-teh ts'oom AH-bent-ess-en.

Serve dinner at nine o'clock.
Servieren Sie das Abendessen um neun Uhr.
sair-VEER'en zee dahss AH-bent-ess-en oom noyn oor.

---

1. Pronounce *ü* like "ee" with your lips in a tight circle.
2. *kh* is a guttural sound.
3. Stress the syllables in capital letters.

🦅 23. A New Type of Dictionary

This dictionary supplies a list of English words with their translation into German. Only one German equivalent is given for each English word—the one most immediately useful to you—so you won't be in doubt regarding which word to use. The phonetic pronunciation is also given for each word so that you will have no difficulty in being understood.

Below we have detailed some suggestions and shortcuts that will enable you to use this dictionary to make hundreds of correct and useful sentences by yourself.

Each German noun is either masculine, feminine, or neuter, and this affects the form of any adjectives and articles that are used in front of it. In the dictionary we have indicated the gender of each noun by putting the proper form of the word "the" in front of it in parentheses: der for masculine nouns, die for feminine, and das for neuter. In the plural, "the" is die before a noun of any gender (when it is used as the subject of a sentence).

In the case of nouns referring to people, we have given two forms—one referring to men and one to women:

the foreigner　(der) Ausländer (a man)
　　　　　　　(die) Ausländerin (a woman)

The plural of nouns, except of a few of foreign origin, is not made with an "s" as in English but by adding one of the endings -e, -er, -n, or -en, and sometimes by changing a simple vowel within the noun to an "umlaut" (ä, ö, or ü). In this dictionary the plural ending for each noun is given after a slash. Thus Wohnung/-en means that the plural of Wohnung is Wohnungen, and Arm/-e that the plural of Arm is Arme. When an umlaut is used, the entire word, or the part of the word in which the umlaut occurs, is repeated for the plural: Kunst/Künste. A dash after the

slash mark means that the plural form of the word is just
the same as the singular: **Keller/—** means that the plural of
Keller is also **Keller** (just as a few English words, such as
"sheep" and "deer," have the same form for the singular
and plural).

Adjectives are used in their simple form without any
special ending when they come after the noun to which
they refer:

The house is small. **Das Haus ist klein.**

When an adjective comes before its noun, either without
an article or with the article **ein** (masculine or neuter) or
eine (feminine), "a," it must take the appropriate masculine, feminine, or neuter ending. These endings, which are
listed for your convenience after each adjective in the
dictionary, are **-er, -e,** and **-es** respectively when the noun
is used as the subject of the sentence.

a small garden	**ein kleiner Garten**
a small apartment	**eine kleine Wohnung**
a small house	**ein kleines Haus**

When the noun is preceded by the article **der, die,** or **das,**
"the," ending of the adjective is **-e** for all three genders.

the small garden	**der kleine Garten**
the small apartment	**die kleine Wohnung**
the small house	**das kleine Haus**

The forms of the articles and the endings of the adjectives also vary when the noun is used as a direct or
indirect object or in the possessive case. You have, no
doubt, already noticed that the endings change in the
phrase book; now you know why. Such case endings
for the articles can be found in the dictionary itself, under
entries like "at the," "to the," "in the," "on the," etc.

The first form of the adjective given in the dictionary is
also the adverb. Both adjectives and adverbs form com-
paratives by adding the ending **-er:**

| quick, *or* quickly | schnell |
| quicker, *or* more quickly | schneller |

Verbs are given in the dictionary in their infinitive form, ending in -en. Observe how the ending of the verb changes according to the subject:

(to) go	gehen
I go (*or* I am going)	ich gehe
you (familiar) go	du gehst
he, she, it goes	er, sie, es geht
we, you (formal), they go	Wir, Sie, sie gehen

(Notice that the same verb form is used with any of the subjects "we," "you," or "they.") Although two forms are given for "you," you should concentrate on using Sie, since it is much more polite than du, which is used within the family, among close friends and students, and to children.

Some of the verbs in the dictionary are followed by (SP) to indicate that they have a separable prefix. These verbs simply "split" when used in forms other than the infinitive. For instance:

| to come in | *herein*kommen (SP) |
| Come in! | Kommen Sie *herein!* |

A detailed study of German verbs is not within the scope of this book. But to help you in making sentences, the present tense of some of the most important verbs—such as "to be," "to have," "to go," "to come," "to want"—is given in this dictionary, as well as some of the most important past pasticiples. In addition, here are some helpful hints to enable you to form sentences with some of the other basic verb forms (tenses and moods), since you have already seen how the present tense is generally formed.

To give an order—use the infinitive form followed by Sie:

| to go | gehen |
| Go! | Gehen Sie! |

To say that you want to do something or to invite someone to do something, use "to want" (**will** or **wollen**) with the infinitive of the second verb:

| I want to go. | **Ich will gehen.** |
| Do you want to go? | **Wollen Sie gehen?** |

For the negative use **nicht** ("not") before the verb:

I do not want to go.   **Ich will nicht gehen.**

And for "would like (to) . . ."—

| I would like (to) . . . | **Ich möchte . . .** |
| Would you like . . . ? | **Möchten Sie . . . ?** |

To express the future, use the present tense of **werden** ("to become") with the infinitive form of the verb:

I will come	**ich werde kommen**
you (familiar) will come	**du wirst kommen**
he, she, it will come	**er, sie, es wird kommen**
we, you (formal), they will come	**wir, Sie, sie werden kommen**

To express something which happened in the past, for most verbs given in the dictionary use the present tense of **haben** ("to have") with the past participle of the verb:

| I had, *or* I have had | **ich habe gehabt** |
| I saw, *or* I have seen | **ich habe gesehen** |

A few verbs require that you use the present tense of **sein** ("to be") with the past participle. These are mostly verbs that express ideas of coming or going, arriving or leaving, etc.:

he went, *or* he has gone   **er ist gegangen**

Since only the most important or irregular past participles are given in the dictionary, note that they are generally formed by adding the prefix **ge-** and changing the ending **-en** of the infinitive to **-t,** or else leaving the **-en** and chang-

ing the internal spelling of the word. (Notice that the past
participle is usually the very last word in the sentence.)

> (to) do   **machen**
> I have done it.   **Ich habe es gemacht.**

> (to) find   **finden**
> She found it.   **Sie hat es gefunden.**

Object pronouns are given within the alphabetical order
of the dictionary. They usually come after the verb, as in
English:

> Tell me.   **Sagen Sie mir.**
> Don't tell him.   **Sagen Sie ihm nicht.**
> I see him.   **Ich sehe ihn.**

The possessive case of proper names follows the English
pattern but without the apostrophe:

> Goethe's works   **Goethes Werke**

The possessive forms of the articles and the pronouns
can be found within the dictionary.

With this advice and the suggestions given in the dictionary, you will be able to use this communicating dictionary
to make up countless sentences on your own and to con-
verse with anyone you may meet.

There is, of course, much more to German grammar
than what we have just mentioned in this introduction.
There are other tenses and moods, strong and weak verbs,
declensions of nouns and adjectives, reflexive pronouns,
etc., as well as numerous idiomatic expressions and various
sayings which reflect the customs, philosophy, and history
of the German-speaking peoples. But you can effectively
use the selected basic vocabulary in this dictionary as an
important step or even springboard to the mastery of
German, and, by means of enthusiastic practice, gradually
absorb and constantly improve your command of this rich
and powerful language.

A

a, an	ein (m), eine (f), ein (n)	*ine, INE-eh, ine*
able	fähig, -er, -e, -es	*FAY-ikh*
about (concerning)	über	*Ü-ber*
above	über	*Ü-ber*
absent	abwesend	*AHP-vay-zent*
accept	annehmen (SP)	*AHN-nay-men*
accident	(der) Unfall /Unfälle	*OON-fahl*
accidentally	zufällig	*ts'oo-FEL-likh*
across	über	*Ü-ber*
actor	(der) Schauspieler/—	*SH'OW-shpeel-er*
actress	(die) Schauspielerin /-nen	*SH'OW-shpeel-er-in*
address	(die) Adresse /-n	*ah-DRESS-eh*
admission	(der) Eintritt/-e	*INE-trit*
advertisement	(die) Anzeige/-n	*AHN-ts'y-ghe*
advise	raten	*RAHT'en*
afraid	bange	*BAHNG-eh*
I am afraid	Ich fürchte mich	*ikh FÜRKH-teh mikh*
Africa	(das) Afrika	*AH-free-ka*

African	afrikanisch, -er, -e, -es	*ah-free-KAHN-ish*
African (person)	(der) Afri-kaner/— (die) Afrika-nerin/-nen	*ah-free-KAHN-er* *ah-free-KAHN-er-in*
after	nach	*nahkh*
afternoon	(der) Nach-mittag/-e	*NAHKH-mit-tahk*
again	wieder	*VEE-der*
against	gegen	*GAY-ghen*
age	(das) Alter	*AHLT-er*
agent	(der) Agent/-en	*ah-ghent*
ago	vor (See how it is used on page 33)	*for*
agree	*über*einstimmen (SP)	*u-ber-INE-shtimm'en*
agreed!	abgemacht!	*AHP-ghe-makht!*
ahead	vorne	*FOR-neh*
air	(die) Luft	*looft*
air conditioning	(die) Klimaan-lage/-en	*KLEE-ma-ahn-la-ghe*
air mail	(die) Luftpost	*LOOFT-post*
airplane	(das) Flug-zeug/-e	*FLOOK-ts'oyk*
airport	(der) Flug-platz/-plätze	*FLOOK-plahtz*
all	alle	*AHL-eh*

That's all!	Das ist alles!	*dahss isst AHL-less!*
allow	erlauben	*air-L'OW-ben*
all right	gut	*goot*
almost	beinahe	*by-NA-eh*
alone	allein	*ahl-LINE*
already	schon	*shohn*
also	auch	*owkh*
(to) alter	ändern	*END-ern*
although	obwohl·	*ohp-VOHL*
always	immer	*IM-mer*
(I) am	(Ich) bin	*(ikh) bin*
America	Amerika	*ah-MAY-ree-ka*
American	amerikanisch, -er, -e, -es	*ah-may-ree-KAHN-ish*
American (person)	(der) Amerikaner/—	*ah-may-ree-KAHN-er*
	(die) Amerikanerin	*ah-may-ree-KAHN-er-in*
amusing	amüsant, -er, -e, -es	*ah-mü-ZAHNT*
and	und	*oont*
angry	böse, -r, —, -s	*BERZ-eh*
animal	(das) Tier/-e	*teer*
ankle	(der) Fußknöchel/—	*FOOSS-kner-khel*
annoying	ärgerlich, -er, -e, -es	*AIR-gher-likh*
answer	(die) Antwort/-en	*AHNT-vort*

(to) answer	antworten	*AHNT-vort'en*
antiseptic (adv & adj)	antiseptisch, -er, -es, -e	*ahn-tee-SEP-tish*
any (of)	etwas	*ET-vahss*
anyone	irgendwer	*eer-ghent-VAIR*
anything	irgend etwas	*eer-ghent et-VAHSS*
anywhere	irgendwo	*EER-ghent-vo*
apartment	(die) Woh- nung/-en	*VO-noong*
appointment	(die) Verabre- dung/-en	*fair-AHP-ray-doong*
April	(der) April	*ahp-REEL*
Arab (person)	(der) Araber/— (die)Arab- erin/-nen	*ah-RAHB-er* *ah-RAHB-er-in*
Arabian	arabisch, -er, -e, -es	*ah-RAHB-ish*
architecture	(die) Archi- tektur	*ar-khee-tek-TOOR*
are		
you (we, they) are	Sie (wir, sie) sind	*zee (veer, zee) zint*
there are	es gibt	*ess ghipt*
arm	(der) Arm/-e	*arm*
army	(die) Armee/-n	*ar-MAY*
around (sur- rounding)	rundherum	*roont-hair-OOM*
around (ap- proximately)	ungefähr	*OON-ghe-fair*

arrival	(die) Ankunft /Ankünfte	*AHN-koonft*
(to) arrive	*an*kommen (SP)	*AHN-kohm'en*
art	(die) Kunst /Künste	*koonst*
artist	(der) Künst-ler/—	*KÜNST-ler*
	(die) Künst-lerin/-nen	*KÜNST-ler-in*
as	wie	*vee*
as (while)	als	*ahlss*
Asia	Asien	*AH-zee-en*
Asian	asiatisch, -er, -e, -es	*ah-zee-AH-tish*
(to) ask	fragen	*FRAHG'en*
aspirin	Aspirin	*ahs-pee-REEN*
assortment	(die) Auswahl /-en	*OWSS-vahl*
at (time)	um	*oom*
at (place)	in	*in*
at the	an dem *or* am (m, n)	*ahn daim, ahm*
	an der	*ahn dair*
	an den	*ahn den*
Atlantic	Atlantik	*aht-LAHN-tick*
Attention!	Achtung!	*AKH-toong!*
August	(der) August	*(dair) OW-goost*
aunt	(die) Tante/-n	*(dee) TAHN-te*

Australia	(das) Australien	*ow-STRA-lee-en*
Australian	australisch, -er, -e, -es	*ow-STRA-lish*
Australian (person)	(der) Austra-lier/—	*ow-STRA-lee-er*
	(die) Austra-lierin/-nen	*ow-STRA-lee-er-in*
Austria	(das) Öster-reich	*ER-ster-ry'kh*
Austrian	österreichisch, -er, -e, -es	*ER-ster-ry'kh-ish*
Austrian (person)	(der) Öster-reicher/—	*ER-ster-ry'kh-er*
	(die) Öster-reicherin /-nen	*ER-ster-ry'kh-er-in*
author	(der) Autor/-en	*ow-TOR*
automatic	automatisch, -er, -e, -es	*ow-toh-MA-tish*
automobile	(das) Auto/-s	*OW-toh*
autumn	(der) Herbst	*hair'pst*
avoid	vermeiden	*fair-MY-den*
away	weg	*veck*

B

baby	(das) Kind-chen/—	*KINT-khen*
bachelor	(der) Jung-geselle/-n	*YOONG-ghe-zel-le*
back (adv.)	zurück	*ts'oo-RÜK*

back (part of the body)	(der) Rücken /–	*RÜK-en*
backwards	rückwärts	*RÜK-vairts*
bad	schlecht	*shlekht*
baggage	(das) Gepäck	*ghe-PAYK*
bandage	(die) Binde/-n	*BIN-deh*
bank	(die) Bank/-en	*bahnk*
bar	(die) Bar/-s	*bar*
barber	(der) Friseur /-e	*free-ZERR*
basement	(der) Keller/–	*KELL-er*
bath	(das) Bad /Bäder	*baht*
bathing suit	(der) Badean- zug/-anzüge	*BA-deh-ahn-ts'ook*
bathroom	(das) Bade- zimmer/–	*BA-deh-ts'im-er*
battery	(die) Batterie /-n	*baht-teh-REE*
battle	(die) Schlacht /-en	*shlakht*
(to) be	sein	*zine*
(See also "am," "is," "are," "was," "were," "been.")		
beach	(der) Strand /Strände	*shtrahnt*
bear	(der) Bär/-en	*bair*
beard	(der) Bart /Bärte	*bahrt*
beautiful	schön	*shern*

beauty	(die) Schön-heit/-en	*SHERN-hite*
beauty parlor	(der) Schön-heitssalon/-s	*SHERN-hites-sah-lohn*
because	weil	*vile*
bed	(das) Bett/-en	*bet*
bedroom	(das) Schlaf-zimmer/—	*SHLAHF-ts'im-er*
beef	(das) Rind-fleisch	*RINT-fly'sh*
been	gewesen	*ghe-VAY-zen*
beer	(das) Bier	*beer*
before (earlier)	vorher	*FOR-hair*
before (in front of, preced-ing)	vor, ehe, bevor	*for, AY-eh, beh-FOR*
(to) begin	*an*fangen (SP)	*AHN-fahng'en*
behind	hinter	*HIN-ter*
(to) believe	glauben	*GL'OWB'en*
Belgium	(das) Belgien	*BEL-ghee-en*
Belgian	belgisch, -er, -e, -es	*BEL-ghish*
Belgian (person)	(der) Belgier/— (die) Belgier-in	*BEL-ghee-er* *BEL-ghee-er-in*
below (prep)	unter	*OON-ter*
below (adv)	unten	*OON-ten*
belt	(der) Gürtel/—	*GUR-tel*
beside	neben	*NAY-ben*

best (adj)	bester, beste, bestes	*BEST-er*
best (adv)	am besten	*ahm BEST-en*
(the) best	(das) Beste	*BEST-eh*
best wishes	(die) Glück-wünsche	*GLÜK-vŭn-sheh*
better	besser, -er, -e, -es	*BESS-er*
between	zwischen	*TS'VISH-en*
bicycle	(das) Fahrrad /-räder	*FAR-raht*
big	groß, größer, -e, -es	*gross*
bill	(die) Rech-nung/-en	*REKH-noong*
bird	(der) Vogel /Vögel	*FOHG-el*
birthday	(der) Geburts-tag/-e	*ghe-BOORTS-tahk*
black	schwarz, -er, -e, -es	*shvartz*
blanket	(die) Bett-decke/-n	*BET-deck-eh*
blood	(das) Blut	*bloot*
blouse	(die) Bluse/-n	*BLOO-zeh*
blue	blau, -er, -e, -es	*bl'ow*
boardinghouse	(die) Pension	*pen-Z'YOHN*
boat	(das) Boot/-e	*boat*
body	(der) Körper/—	*KERP-er*

book	(das) Buch /Bücher	*bookh*
bookstore	(die) Buchhand- lung/-en	*BOOKH-hahnd-loong*
born	geboren	*ghe-BORE'en*
(to) borrow	borgen	*BORG'en*
boss	(der) Chef/-s	*shef*
both	beide	*BY-deh*
(to) bother	stören	*SHTERR'en*
bottle	(die) Flasche /-n	*FLA-sheh*
bottom	(der) Boden /Böden	*BO-den*
bought	gekauft	*ghe-KOWFT*
bowl	(die) Schüs- sel/-n	*SHÜ-sel*
boy	(der) Knabe/-n	*K'NAHB-eh*
brain	(das) Gehirn	*ghe-HEERN*
brake	(die) Bremse/-n	*BREM-ze*
brave	tapfer, -er, -e, -es	*TAHP-fer*
bread	(das) Brot/-e	*broht*
(to) break	brechen	*BREHKH'en*
breakfast	(das) Früh- stück/-e	*FRÜ-shtŭk*
bridge	(die) Brücke/-n	*BRÜ-keh*
bridge (card game)	(das) Bridge- spiel/-e	*BRIDGE-shpeel*

briefcase	(die) Akten-tasche/-n	*AHKT-en-ta-sheh*
(to) bring	bringen	*BRING'en*
Bring me . . . (something)	Bringen Sie mir . . .	*BRING'en zee meer . . .*
broken	gebrochen	*ghe-BROKH'en*
brother	(der) Bruder /Brüder	*BROOD-er*
brother-in-law	(der) Schwager /Schwäger	*SHVA-gher*
brown	braun, -er, -e,-es	*brown*
brush	(die) Bürste/-n	*(dee) BÜR-steh*
building	(das) Ge-bäude/—	*ghe-BOY-de*
bureau	(das) Büro/-s	*bü-RO*
bus	(der) Bus/-e	*booss*
bus stop	(die) Bushal-testelle/-n	*BOOSS-hahl-teh-shtel-eh*
business	(das) Ge-schäft/-e	*ghe-SHEFT*
busy	beschäftigt	*beh-SHEFT-ikht*
but	aber	*AH-ber*
butter	(die) Butter	*BOOT-ter*
button	(der) Knopf /Knöpfe	*k'nopf*
(to) buy	kaufen	*KOWF'en*
by (near)	bei	*by*
by (agent)	von	*fohn*

C

cabbage	(der) Kohl	*kohl*
cake	(der) Kuchen/—	*KOO-khen*
(to) call	rufen	*ROOF'en*
(to) call (tele-phone)	*an*rufen (SP)	*AHN-roof'en*
Call me!	Rufen Sie mich an!	*ROOF'en zee mikh ahn!*
calm	ruhig, -er, -e, -es	*ROO-ikh*
camera	(die) Ka-mera/-s	*KA-meh-ra*
can (to be able to)	können	*KERN'en*
Can you . . . ?	Können Sie . . . ?	*KERN'en zee . . . ?*
I can	ich kann	*ikh kahn*
I can't	ich kann nicht	*ikh kahn nikht*
can (container)	(die) Büchse/-n	*BÜK-seh*
can opener	(der) Büchsen-öffner/—	*BÜK-sen-erf-ner*
capable	fähig, -er, -e, -es	*FAY-ikh*
captain (sea)	(der) Kapitän /-e	*ka-pee-TAIN*
captain (police, army)	(der) Haupt-mann /-männer	*HOWPT-mahn*
car	(der) Wagen/—	*VA-ghen*

carburetor	(der) Ver- gaser/—	*fer-GA-zer*
card	(die) Karte/-n	*KAR-teh*
careful	vorsichtig, -er, -e, -es	*FOR-zikh-tikh*
(Be) careful!	(Seien Sie) vor- sichtig!	*ZY'en zee FOR-zikh- tikh!*
care	(die) Sorge/-n	*ZOR-ghe*
carrot	(die) Karot- te/-n	*ka-ROHT-eh*
(to) carry	tragen	*TRAHG'en*
Carry this to . . . !	Tragen Sie dies zu . . . !	*TRAHG'en zee deess ts'oo . . . !*
castle	(das) Schloß/ Schlösser	*shlohss*
cat	(die) Katze/-n	*KAHT-ts'eh*
cathedral	(der) Dom/-e	*dohm*
catholic	katholisch, -er, -e, -es	*ka-TOH-lish*
cellar	(der) Keller/—	*KELL-er*
cemetery	(der) Fried- hof/-höfe	*FREED-hohf*
center	(das) Zent- rum/-s	*TS'ENT-room*
centimeter	(der) Zenti- meter/—	*ts'en-tee-MAYT-er*
century	(das) Jahrhun- dert/-e	*yahr-HOON-dert*
certainly	sicherlich	*ZIKH-er-likh*

chair	(der) Stuhl/ Stühle	*shtool*
chandelier	(der) Kronleuchter/—	*KROHN-loy'kh-ter*
change	(der) Wechsel/—	*VEX-el*
change (money)	(das) Wechselgeld	*VEX-el-ghelt*
(to) change	wechseln	*VEX-eln*
charming	scharmant, -er, -e, -es	*shar-MAHNT*
chauffeur	(der) Fahrer/—	*FAR-er*
cheap	billig, -er, -e, -es	*BILL-ikh*
check (money)	(der) Scheck/-s	*shek*
(baggage) check	(der) Gepäckschein/-e	*ghe-PAYK-shine*
checkroom	(die) Garderobe/-n	*gar-deh-RO-beh*
cheese	(der) Käse	*KAYZ-eh*
chest	(die) Brust/ Brüste	*broost*
chicken	(das) Hühnchen/—	*HÜN-khen*
child	(das) Kind/-er	*kint*
China	(das) China	*KHEE-nah*
Chinese	chinesisch, -er, -e, -es	*khee-NAY-zish*
Chinese (person)	(der) Chinese/-n	*khee-NAY-zeh*
	(die) Chinesin/-nen	*khee-NAY-zin*

chocolate	(die) Schoko-lade	*sho-ko-LA-deh*
church	(die) Kirche/-en	*KEER-kheh*
cigar	(die) Zi-garre/-n	*ts'ee-GAR-eh*
cigarette	(die) Zi-garette/-n	*ts'ee-gar-ET-eh*
city	(die) Stadt/Städte	*shtaht*
clean	rein, -er, -e, -es	*rine*
(to) clean	reinigen	*RINE-ig'en*
clear	klar, -er, -e, -es	*klahr*
clever	gescheit, -er, -e, -es	*ghe-SHITE*
clock	(die) Uhr/-en	*oor*
close (near)	nahe	*NA-eh*
(to) close	schließen	*SHLEESS'en*
closed	geschlossen	*ghe-SHLOHSS'en*
clothes	(die) Kleider	*KLY-der*
coast	(die) Küste/-n	*KÜ-ste*
coat (suit)	(der) Kittel/—	*KIT-el*
(overcoat)	(der) Mantel/Mäntel	*MAHN-tel*
coffee	(der) Kaffee	*KA-fay*
cold (sickness)	(die) Erkält-ung/-en	*air-KELT-oong*
cold	kalt, -er, -e, -es	*kahlt*
colonel	(der) Oberst/-e	*OH-berst*

color	(die) Farbe/-n	*FAR-beh*
(to) come	kommen	*KOHM'en*
I come	ich komme	*KOHM-eh*
he (she, it) comes	er (sie, es) kommt	*kohmt*
you (we, they) come	Sie (wir, sie) kommen	*KOHM'en*
Come (here)!	Kommen Sie (her)!	*KOHM'en zee (hair)!*
Come in!	Kommen Sie herein!	*KOHM'en zee hair-INE!*
(to) come back	*zurück*kommen (SP)	*ts'oo-RÜK-kohm'en*
comb	(der) Kamm/ Kämme	*kahm*
company (business)	(die) Gesell- schaft/-en	*ghe-ZELL-shahft*
competition	(die) Konkur- renz	*kohn-koor-ENTS*
complete	vollständig, -er, -e, -es	*FOHL-shtend-ikh*
computer	(der) com- puter/—	*kohm-POO-ter*
concert	(das) Kon- zert/-e	*kon-TS'AIRT*
(to) congratulate	gratulieren	*gra-too-LEER'en*
contract	(der) Vertrag/ Verträge	*fair-TRAHK*
conversation	(die) Unter- haltung/-en	*oon-ter-HAHLT-oong*

cook	(der) Koch/ Köche	*kohkh*
(to) cook	kochen	*KO-khen*
cool	kühl, -er, -e, -es	*kůl*
copy	(die) Kopie/-n	*ko-PEE*
corner	(die) Ecke/-n	*EK-eh*
correct	richtig, -er, -e, -es	*RIKH-tikh*
(to) cost	kosten	*KOHST'en*
cotton	(die) Baum- wolle/-n	*B'OWM-vohl-eh*
cough	(der) Husten	*HOO-sten*
country	(das) Land/ Länder	*lahnt*
cousin	(der) Vetter/-n (die) Kusine/-n	*FET-er* *koo-ZEE-neh*
cow	(die) Kuh/ Kühe	*koo*
crazy	verrückt, -er, -e, -es	*fair-RÜKT*
(to) cross	überqueren	*ů-ber-KVAIR'en*
cup	(die) Tasse/-n	*TAHSS-eh*
customs (office, fee)	(der) Zoll	*ts'ohl*
customs form	(das) Zollfor- mular/-e	*TS'OHL-for-moo-lar*
(to) cut	schneiden	*SHNY-den*

Czech (person)	(der) Tsche-che/-n	*CHEH-kheh*
	(die) Tsche-chin/-nen	*CHEH-khin*
Czechoslovakia	(die) Tsche-choslowakei	*cheh-kho-slo-va-KYE*
Czechoslova-kian	tschechoslo-wakisch, -er. -e, -es	*cheh-kho-slo-VA-kish*

D

(to) dance	tanzen	*TAHNTS'en*
dangerous	gefährlich, -er, -e, -es	*ghe-FAIR-likh*
dark	dunkel, dunkler, dunkle, dunkles	*DOONK-el*
date (calendar)	(das) Datum/ Daten	*DA-toom*
date (appoint-ment)	(die) Verabre-dung/-en	*fair-AHP-ray-doong*
daughter	(die) Tochter/ Töchter	*TOKH-ter*
day	(der) Tag/-e	*tahk*
dead	tot, -er, -e, -es	*toht*
dear	lieb, -er, -e, -es	*leep*
(my) dear	(mein) Liebling	*LEEB-ling*
December	(der) Dezember	*deh-TS'EM-ber*
(to) decide	entscheiden	*ent-SHY-den*

deep	tief, -er, -e, -es	*teef*
delay	(die) Verzöge-rung/-en	*fair-TS'ERG-er-oong*
delighted	sehr erfreut	*zair er-FROYT*
delicious	köstlich, -er, -e, -es	*KERST-likh*
dentist	(der) Zahn-arzt/-ärzte	*TS'AHN-artst*
department store	(das) Waren-haus/-häuser	*VAR-en-howss*
desk	(der) Schreib-tisch/-e	*SHRIPE-tish*
detour	(die) Um-leitung/-en	*OOM-lite-oong*
devil	(der) Teufel/—	*TOY-fel*
dictionary	(das) Wörter-buch/-bücher	*VERT-er-bookh*
different (one)	anderer, an-dere, anderes	*AHN-der-er*
difficult	schwierig, -er, -e, -es	*SHVEE-rikh*
(to) dine	speisen	*SHPY-zen*
dining room	(das) Eßzim-mer/—	*ESS-ts'im-er*
dinner	(das) Abend-essen/—	*AH-bent-ess-en*
direction	(die) Rich-tung/-en	*RIKH-toong*
dirty	schmutzig, -er, -e, -es	*SHMOO-ts'ikh*

disappointed	enttäuscht	*ent-TOYSHT*
discount	(der) Rabatt/-e	*RAHB-aht*
divorced	geschieden	*ghe-SHEED'en*
dizzy	schwindlig, -er, -e, -es	*SHVIND-likh*
(to) do	tun	*toon*

"Do" is not used to ask a question or to form the negative. For a question, simply put the subject after the verb; and for the negative, use **nicht** after the verb.

Do you understand?	Verstehen Sie?	*fair-SHTAY'en zee?*
I don't have	Ich habe nicht	*ikh HA-beh nikht*
Don't go!	Gehen Sie nicht!	*GAY'en zee nikht!*
Don't do that!	Tun Sie das nicht!	*toon zee dahss nikht!*
doctor	(der) Arzt/ Ärzte	*artst*
dog	(der) Hund/-e	*hoont*
dollar	(der) Dollar/-s	*DOH-lar*
door	(die) Tür/-en	*tür*
(already) done	(schon) gemacht	*(shohn) ghe-MAKHT*
donkey	(der) Esel/—	*AYZ-el*
down (direction)	herunter	*hair-OONT-er*
down (location)	unten	*OON-ten*
dress	(das) Kleid/-er	*klite*

(to) drink	trinken	*TRINK'en*
(to) drive	fahren	*FAR'en*
driver	(der) Fahrer/—	*FAR-er*
driver's license	(der) Führer- schein/-e	*FÜR-er-shine*
drunk	betrunken	*beh-TROONK'en*
Dutch	holländisch, -er, -e, -es	*HO-lend-ish*
Dutchman	(der) Hollän- der/—	*HO-lend-er*
Dutch woman	(die) Hollän- derin/-nen	*HO-lend-er-in*

E

each	jeder, jede, jedes	*YEH-der*
ear	(das) Ohr/-en	*ohr*
early	früh, -er, -e, -es	*frü*
(to) earn	verdienen	*fair-DEEN'en*
earth	(die) Erde	*AIR-deh*
east	(der) Osten	*OHST-en*
(to) eat	essen	*ESS'en*
egg	(das) Ei/-er	*eye*
eight	acht	*ahkht*
eighteen	achtzehn	*AHKH-ts'ayn*
eighty	achtzig	*AHKH-ts'ikh*
either . . . or	entweder . . . oder	*ent-VAY-der . . . O-der*

electric	elektrisch	*el-EKT-rish*
elephant	(der) Elefant/ -en	*el-ef-AHNT*
elevator	(der) Aufzug/ Aufzüge	*OWF-ts'ook*
eleven	elf	*elf*
else (more)	noch	*nokh*
(or) else	sonst	*zonst*
embassy	(die) Bot- schaft/-en	*BOAT-shahft*
emergency	(die) Not- lage/-n	*NOHT-la-gheh*
employee	(der, die) An- gestellte/-n	*AHN-ghe-shtel-teh*
employer	.(der) Arbeit- geber/—	*AR-bite-gay-ber*
end	(das) Ende/-n	*EN-de*
(to) end	enden	*END'en*
England	(das) England	*ENG-lahnt*
English	englisch, -er, -e, -es	*ENG-lish*
Englishman	(der) Englän- der/—	*ENG-len-der*
English- woman	(die) Englän- derin/-nen	*ENG-len-der-in*
entertaining	unterhaltend, -er, -e, -es	*oon-ter-HAHLT-ent*
error	(der) Fehler/—	*FAIL-er*

especially	besonders	*beh-ZOHND-ers*
European	europäisch, -er, -e, -es	*eh-oo-ro-PAY-ish*
European (person)	(der) Europäer/—	*eh-oo-ro-PAY-er*
	(die) Europäerin/-nen	*eh-oo-ro-PAY-er-in*
evening	(der) Abend/-e	*AH-bent*
ever (sometimes)	manchmal	*MAHNKH-mahl*
every	jeder, jede, jedes	*YEH-der*
everybody	alle	*AH-le*
everything	alles	*AH-less*
exact	genau, -er, -e, -es	*ghe-NOW*
excellent	ausgezeichnet, -er, -e, -es	*OWSS-ghe-ts'ykh-net*
except	außer	*OW-ser*
(to) exchange	*um*wechseln (SP)	*OOM-vex-eln*
Excuse me!	Entschuldigung!	*ent-SHOOL-dee-goong*
exit	(der) Ausgang/Ausgänge	*OWSS-gahng*
expensive	teuer, -er, -e, -es	*TOY-er*
experience	(die) Erfahrung/-en	*air-FAR-oong*

explanation	(die) Erklär- ung/-en	*air-KLAIR-oong*
(to) export	exportieren	*ex-por-TEER'en*
extra	extra	*EX-tra*
eye	(das) Auge/-n	*OW-ghe*

F

face	(das) Ge- sicht/-er	*ghe-ZIKHT*
factory	(die) Fa- brik/-en	*fa-BREEK*
fair (village)	(der) Jahr- markt/ -märkte	*YAR-markt*
fall (autumn)	(der) Herbst	*hairpst*
fall (drop)·	(der) Sturz/ Stürze	*shtoorts*
(to) fall	fallen	*FAHL'en*
family	(die) Fami- lie/-n	*fa-MEE-lee-yeh*
famous	berühmt, -er, -e, -es	*beh-RÜMT*
far	weit	*vite*
How far?	Wie weit?	*vee vite?*
farm	(der) Bauern- hof/-höfe	*B'OW-ern-hohf*
farther	weiter	*VITE-er*

fast	schnell, -er, -e, -es	*shnel*
fat	dick, -er, -e, -es	*dick*
father	(der) Vater/ Väter	*FA-ter*
February	(der) Februar	*FAY-broo-ar*
(to) feel	fühlen	*FÜ-len*
fever	(das) Fieber/—	*FEE-ber*
few	wenig	*VAY-nikh*
fifteen	fünfzehn	*FÜNF-ts'ayn*
fifty	fünfzig	*FÜNF-ts'ikh*
(to) fight	kämpfen	*KEMP-fen*
(to) fill	füllen	*FÜL'en*
film	(der) Film/-e	*feelm*
finally	endlich	*END-likh*
(to) find	finden	*FIN-den*
(to) find out	*heraus*finden (SP)	*hair-OWSS-fin-den*
finger	(der) Finger/—	*FING-er*
(to) finish	beenden	*beh-END'en*
fire	(das) Feuer/—	*FOY-er*
first	erst, -er, -e, -es	*airst*
(to) fish	fischen	*FISH'en*
five	fünf	*fünf*
flight	(der) Flug/ Flüge	*flook*

floor (of building)	(der) Stock/ Stöcke	*shtohk*
flower	(die) Blume/-n	*BLOOM-eh*
(to) fly	fliegen	*FLEEG'en*
fly (insect)	(die) Fliege/-n	*FLEE-gheh*
food	(das) Essen	*ESS-en*
foot	(der) Fuß/ Füße	*fooss*
for	für	*für*
foreigner	(der) Ausländer/—	*OWSS-lend-er*
	(die) Ausländerin/-nen	*OWSS-lend-er-in*
(to) forget	vergessen	*'fair-GUESS'en*
Don't forget!	Nicht vergessen!	*nikht fair-GUESS'en!*
fork	(die) Gabel/-n	*GA-bel*
forty	vierzig	*FEER-ts'ikh*
fountain	(der) Springbrunnen/—	*SHPRING-broon-en*
four	vier	*feer*
fourteen	vierzehn	*FEER-ts'ayn*
fox	(der) Fuchs/ Füchse	*foox*
France	(das) Frankreich	*FRAHNK-ry'kh*
free	frei, -er, -e, -es	*fry*
French	franzözisch, -er, -e, -es	*frahn-TS'ER-zish*

Frenchman	(der) Franzo-ze/-n	*frahn-TS'OH-zeh*
French woman	(die) Französin/-nen	*frahn-TS'ER-zin*
frequently	oft	*ohft*
fresh	frisch, -er, -e, -es	*frish*
Friday	(der) Freitag/-e	*FRY-tahk*
fried	gebraten, -er, -e, -es	*ghe-BRAHT'en*
friend	(der) Freund/-e (die) Freundin/-nen	*froynt* *FROYN-din*
from	von	*fohn*
from the	von dem or vom (m, n)	*fohn daim, fohm*
	von der (f)	*fohn dair*
	von den (pl)	*fohn dain*
(in) front of	vor	*fohr*
fruit	(die) Frucht/ Früchte	*frookht*
full	voll, -er, -e, -es	*fohl*
funny	komisch, -er, -e, -es	*KOHM-ish*
future	(die) Zukunft	*TS'OO-koonft*

G

game	(das) Spiel/-e	*shpeel*
garden	(der) Garten/ Gärten	*GAR-ten*

gasoline	(das) Benzin	*ben-TS'EEN*
gas station	(die) Tank-stelle/-n	*TAHNK-shtel-eh*
garage	(die) Garage/-n	*gar-AH-zheh*
general	allgemein, -er, -e, -es	*AHL-gheh-mine*
general (military)	(der) General/Generäle	*gheh-neh-RAHL*
gentlemen!	(meine) Herr-schaften!	*(MINE-eh) HAIR-shahft-en!*
genuine	echt, -er, -e, -es	*ekht*
German	deutsch, -er, -e, -es	*doych*
German (person)	(der, die) Deutsche/-n	*DOYCH-eh*
Germany	(das) Deutsch-land	*DOYCH-lahnt*
(to) get	bekommen	*beh-KOHM'en*
(to) get off	*aus*steigen (SP)	*OWSS-shty-ghen*
(to) get on (into)	*ein*steigen (SP)	*INE-shty-ghen*
(to) get up	*auf*stehen (SP)	*OWF-shtay'en*
(to) get up (on something)	*auf*steigen (SP)	*OWF-shty-ghen*
Get out!	Raus!	*R'OWSS!*
Give me ...	Geben Sie mir ..	*GAY-ben zee meer ...*

(to) give	geben	*GAY-ben*
girl	(das) Mäd-chen/–	*MAYT-yen*
glass	(das) Glas/ Gläser	*glahss*
(eye)glasses	(die) Brille/-n	*BRIL-leh*
glove	(der) Hand- schuh/-e	*HAHNT-shoo*
(to) go	gehen	*GAY'en*
I go	ich gehe	*GAY-eh*
he (she, it) goes	er (sie, es) geht	*gait*
you (we, they) go	Sie (wir, sie) gehen	*GAY'en*
(to) go away	weggehen (SP)	*VEK-gay'en*
Go away!	Gehen Sie weg!	*GAY'en zee vek!*
(to) go back	zurückgehen (SP)	*ts'oo-RÜK-gay'en*
(to) go on	weitergehen (SP)	*VITE-er-gay'en*
Go on!	Gehen Sie weiter!	*GAY'en zee VITE-er!*
God	(der) Gott/ Götter	*goht*
gold	(das) Gold	*golt*
good	gut	*goot*
Goodbye!	Auf Wieder- sehen!	*owf VEE-dair-zay'en*
government	(die) Regier- ung/-en	*reh-GEER-oong*
grandfather	(der) Groß- vater/-väter	*GROHSS-fa-ter*

grandmother	(die) Groß-mutter/-mütter	*GROHSS-moot-er*
grateful	dankbar,-er,-e,-es	*DAHNK-bar*
gray	grau	*gr'ow*
great	groß,-er,-e,-es	*gross*
a great many	sehr viele	*zair FEEL-eh*
Greece	(das) Griechen-land	*GREE-khen-lahnt*
Greek	griechisch,-er,-e,-es	*GREE-khish*
Greek (person)	(der) Grie-che/-n (die) Grie-chin/-nen	*GREE-kheh* *GREE-khin*
green	grün,-er,-e,-es	*grün*
gross (weight)	Brutto	*BROOT-toh*
group	(die) Gruppe/-n	*GROOP-eh*
guide	(der) Reise-führer/—	*RY-zeh-für-er*
guitar	(die) Gi-tarre/-n	*ghee-TAR-eh*

H

hair	(das) Haar/-e	*har*
hairbrush	(die) Haar-bürste/-n	*HAR-bür-steh*
haircut	(der) Haar-schnitt/-e	*HAR-shnit*
half	halb,-er,-e,-es	*hahlp*
hand	(die) Hand/Hände	*hahnt*
happy	glücklich,-er,-e,-es	*GLÜK-likh*

hat	(der) Hut/ Hüte	*hoot*
(to) have	haben	*HAHB'en*
I have	ich habe	*HAHB-eh*
he (she, it) has	er (sie, es) hat	*haht*
you (we, they) have	Sie (wir, sie) haben	*HAHB'en*
Have you . . . ?	Haben Sie . . . ?	*HAHB'en zee . . . ?*
he	er	*air*
head	(der) Kopf	*kohpf*
heart	(das) Herz/-en	*hair'ts*
heavy	schwer, -er, -e, -es	*shvair*
(to) hear	hören	*HER'en*
Hello! (phone)	Hallo!	*HA-lo!*
(to) help	helfen	*HELF'en*
Help!	Hilfe!	*HEEL-feh!*
her (direct object)	sie	*zee*
(to) her	ihr	*eer*
her (possessive)	ihr (m), ihre (f), ihr (n); ihre (pl)	*eer, EER-eh*
here	hier	*heer*
high	hoch, hoher, hohe, hohes	*hohkh, HO-er*

higher	höher, -er, -e, -es	*HER-er*
highway	(die) Auto-bahn/-en	*OW-toh-bahn*
hill	(der) Hügel/—	*HÜG-el*
him	ihn	*een*
(to) him	ihm	*eem*
his	sein (m), seine (f), sein (n); seine (pl)	*ZINE, ZINE-eh*
history	(die) Ge-schichte/-n	*ghe-SHIKH-teh*
Holland	(das) Holland	*HO-lahnt*
(at) home	zu Hause	*ts'oo HOW-zeh*
horse	(das) Pferd/-e	*pfairt*
hospital	(das) Kranken-haus/-häuser	*KRAHNK-en-howss*
hot	heiß, -er, -e, -es	*hice*
hotel	(das) Hotel/-s	*ho-TEL*
hour	(die) Stunde/-n	*SHTOON-deh*
house	(das) Haus/ Häuser	*howss*
how	wie	*vee*
however	jedoch	*yeh-DOHKH*
hundred	hundert	*HOON-dert*
Hungary	(das) Ungarn	*OON-garn*
Hungarian	ungarisch, -er, -e, -es	*OON-gar-ish*

Hungarian (person)	(der) Ungar/ -en	*OON-gar*
	(die) Ungarin/ -nen	*OON-gar-in*
hungry	hungrig, -er -e, -es	*HOONG-rikh*
(to) hurry	eilen	*EYE-len*
Hurry up!	Beeilen Sie sich!	*beh-EYE-len zee zikh!*
husband	(der) Mann/ Männer	*mahn*

I

I	ich	*ikh*
ice	(das) Eis	*ice*
ice cream	(das) Eis	*ice*
idiot	(der) Idiot/-en	*ee-d'yoht*
if	wenn	*ven*
imagine	sich *vorstellen* (SP)	*zikh FOR-shtel'en*
Just imagine!	Stellen Sie sich vor!	*SHTEL'en zee zikh for!*
(to) import	importieren	*im-port-EER'en*
important	wichtig, -er, -e, -es	*VIKH-tikh*
impossible	unmöglich, -er, -e, -es	*OON-merg-likh*
in	in	*in*

in the	in dem *or* im (m, n)	*in daim, im*
	in der (f)	*in dair*
	in den (pl)	*in dain*
including	einschließlich	*INE-shlees-likh*
industry	(die) Indu-strie/-n	*in-doo-STREE*
information	(die) Auskunft	*OWSS-koonft*
inn	(die) Gast-stätte/-n	*GAHST-shtet-eh*
inquiry	(die) Erkundi-gung/-en	*air-KOON-dee-goong*
inside	innen *or* drin	*IN-en, drin*
instead	anstatt	*ahn-SHTAHT*
intelligent	intelligent, -er, -e, -es	*in-tel-ee-GHENT*
interested	interessiert, -er, -e, -es	*in-tair-ess-EERT*
interesting	interessant, -er, -e, -es	*in-tair-ess-AHNT*
interpreter	(der) Dol-metscher/—	*DOHL-meh-cher*
into the	in den (m)	*in dain*
	in die (f)	*in dee*
	in das *or* ins (n)	*in dahss, inss*
	in die (pl)	*in dee*
(to) introduce	vorstellen (SP)	*FOR-shtel'en*
May I intro-duce . . .	Darf ich vor-stellen . . .	*darf ikh FOR-shtel'-en . . .*

invitation	(die) Einla-dung/-en	*INE-la-doong*
(he, she, it) is	(er, sie, es) ist	*isst*
there is	es gibt	*ess ghipt*
island	(die) Insel/-n	*IN-zel*
it	es	*ess*
it is	es ist	*ess isst*
its	sein (m), seine (f), sein (n); seine (pl)	*zine, ZINE-eh*
Italian	italienisch, -er, -e, -es	*ee-tahl-YEH-nish*
Italian (person)	(der) Italie-ner/—	*ee-tahl-YEH-ner*
	(die) Italiener-in/-nen	*ee-tahl-YEH-ner-in*
Italy	(das) Italien	*ee-TA-lee-yen*

J

jacket	(die) Jacke/-n	*YA-keh*
January	(der) Januar	*YA-noo-ar*
Japan	(das) Japan	*YA-pahn*
Japanese	japanisch, -er, -e, -es	*ya-PAHN-ish*
Japanese (per-son)	(der) Ja-paner/—	*ya-PAHN-er*
	(die) Japaner-in/-nen	*ya-PAHN-er-in*

jewelry	(der) Schmuck	*shmook*
Jewish	jüdisch, -er, -e, -es	*YŪ-dish*
job	(die) Arbeit/-en	*AR-bite*
joke	(der) Witz/-e	*vitz*
(to) joke	scherzen	*SHAIR-ts'en*
July	(der) Juli	*YOO-lee*
June	(der) Juni	*YOO-nee*
just (only)	nur	*noor*
just (now)	eben	*AY-ben*

K

(to) keep	behalten	*beh-HAHLT'en*
Keep out!	Eintritt verboten!	*INE-trit fair-BO-ten!*
key	(der) Schlüssel/—	*SHLŪS-sel*
kind	liebenswürdig, -er, -e, -es	*LEE-benss-vûr-dikh*
king	(der) König/-e	*KERN-ig*
kiss	(der) Kuß/ Küße	*kooss*
kitchen	(die) Küche/-n	*KŪ-khe*
knee	(das) Knie/—	*k'nee*
knife	(das) Messer/—	*MESS-er*
(to) know (a fact)	wissen	*VISS'en*

(to) know (to be acquainted with)	kennen	*KEN'en*
(to) know how	können	*KERN'en*
Do you know . . . ?	Wissen Sie . . . ?	*VISS'en zee?*
Who knows?	Wer weiß?	*vair vice?*

L

ladies' room	(die) Damen-toilette/-en	*DA-men-twa-let-eh*
ladies and gentlemen!	Meine Damen und Herren!	*MINE-eh DAHM-en oont hair'n!*
lady	(die) Dame/-n	*DAH-meh*
lake	(der) See/-n	*zay*
lamb	(das) Lamm/ Lämmer	*lahm*
land	(das) Land/ Länder	*lahnt*
language	(die) Spra-che/-n	*SHPRAH-khe*
large	groß, -er, -e, -es	*grohss*
larger	größer, -er, -e, -es	*GRERSS-er*
last	letzt, -er, -e, -es	*LETST*
late	spät, -er, -e, -es	*shpayt*
later	später	*SHPAYT-er*

lawyer	(der) Rechtsan-walt/-an-wälte	*REKHTS-ahn-vahlt*
(to) learn	lernen	*LAIRN'en*
leather	(das) Leder	*LAID-er*
(to) leave	verlassen	*fair-LAHSS'en*
left (direction)	links	*links*
leg	(das) Bein/-e	*bine*
lemon	(die) Zi-trone/-n	*ts'it-RO-ne*
(to) lend	verleihen	*fair-LY'en*
less	weniger	*VAY-nig-er*
lesson	(die) Stunde/-n	*SHTOON-deh*
(to) let (permit)	lassen	*LAHSS'en*
Let us ...	Lassen Sie uns ...	*LAHSS'en zee oonss ...*
Let's go!	Gehen wir!	*GAY'en veer!*
letter (mail)	(der) Brief/-e	*breef*
lettuce	(der) Kopfsa-lat	*KOHPF-za-laht*
liberty	(die) Freiheit/-en	*FRY-hite*
lieutenant	(der) Leut-nant/-s	*LOYT-nahnt*
life	(das) Leben	*LAYB-en*
(to) lift	*auf*heben (SP)	*OWF-hayb'en*
light (weight)	leicht, -er, -e, -es	*ly'kht*

light (illumination)	(das) Licht/-er	*likht*
like	wie	*vee*
Like this.	Wie das.	*vee dahss.*
(to) like	gerne haben	*GAIR-neh HAHB'en*
lion	(der) Löwe/-n	*LERV-eh*
lip	(die) Lippe/-n	*LIP-eh*
list	(die) Liste/-n	*LIST-eh*
(to) listen	zuhören (SP)	*TS'OO-her'en*
little (small)	klein, -er, -e, -es	*kline*
a little	ein bißchen	*ine BISS-yen*
(to) live	leben	*LAYB'en*
living room	(das) Wohnzimmer/—	*VOHN-ts'im-er*
long	lang, -er, -e, -es	*lahng*
(to) look	schauen	*SH'OW'en*
Look out!	Gib acht!	*ghip ahkht!.*
(to) lose	verlieren	*fair-LEER'en*
lost	verloren	*fair-LOHR'en*
lost and found office	(das) Fundbüro/-s	*FOONT-bü-ro*
(a) lot	viel	*feel*
(to) love	lieben	*LEE-ben*
low	niedrig, -er, -e, -es	*NEED-rikh*

luck	(das) Glück	*glûk*
Good luck!	Viel Glück!	*feel glûk*
bad luck	(das) Pech	*paykh*
luggage	(das) Gepäck	*ghe-PAIK*
lunch	(das) Mittag-essen/—	*MIT-tahk-ess-en*

M

machine	(die) Ma-schine/-n	*mah-SHEE-neh*
madam	gnädige Frau	*GNAY-dee-ghe FR'OW*
made	gemacht, -er, -e, -es,	*ghe-MAKHT*
maid (servant)	(das) Dienst-mädchen/—	*DEENST-mayt-yen*
mailbox	(der) Brief-kasten/—	*BREEF-kahst-en*
(to) make	machen	*MAKH'en*
man	(der) Mann/ Männer	*mahn*
manager	(der) Verwal-ter/-wälter	*fair-VAHL-ter*
many	viele	*FEEL-eh*
map	(die) Karte/-n	*KAR-te*
March	(der) März	*mairts*
market	(der) Markt/ Märkte	*markt*
married	verheiratet	*fair-HI-raht-et*

mass (religious)	(die) Messe/-n	*MESS-eh*
match (for fire)	(das) Streich-holz/-hölzer	*SHTRY'KH-hohlts*
(What's the) matter?	Was ist los?	*vahss isst lohss?*
May I?	Darf ich?	*darf ikh?*
May	(der) Mai	*my*
maybe	vielleicht	*feel-LY'KHT*
me	mich	*mikh*
(to) me	mir	*meer*
(to) mean	meinen	*MINE-en*
meat	(das) Fleisch	*fly'sh*
mechanic	(der) Mecha-niker/—	*meh-KHAHN-ik-er*
medicine	(die) Medizin/-en	*meh-dee-TS'EEN*
Mediterranean	(das) Mittel-meer	*MIT-el-mair*
(to) meet	treffen	*TREF'en*
meeting	(das) Zusamen-treffen/—	*ts'oo-ZAHM-en-tref'en*
member	(das) Mit-glied/-er	*MIT-gleet*
(to) mend	reparieren	*ray-par-EER'en*
men	(die) Männer	*MEN-er*
men's room	(die) Herren-toilette/-n	*HAIR-en-twa-let-eh*

menu	(die) Speise- karte/-n	*SHPY-zeh-kar-teh*
message	(die) Mitteil- ung/-en	*MIT-tile-oong*
Mexican	mexikanisch, -er, -e, -es	*mex-ih-KA-nish*
Mexican (per- son)	(der) Mexika- ner/—	*mex-ih-KA-ner*
	(die) Mexika- nerin/-nen	*mex-ih-KA-ner-in*
middle	(die) Mitte/-n	*MIT-eh*
in the middle	mitten drin	*MIT-en drin*
middle (adj)	mittler, -er, -e, -es	*MIT-ler*
mile	(die) Meile/-n	*MILE-eh*
milk	(die) Milch	*meelkh*
million	(die) Million/ -en	*MEEL-yohn*
minister (clergy)	(der) Geistliche	*GHY'ST-lee-kheh*
minute	(die) Minute/-n	*mee-NOO-teh*
Miss	(das) Fräu- lein/—	*FROY-line*
(to) miss (emo- tion)	vermissen	*fair-MISS'en*
(to) miss (a train, etc.)	verpassen	*fair-PAHSS'en*
mistake	(der) Fehler/—	*FAY-ler*
misunderstand- ing	(das) Mißver- ständnis/-se	*MISS-fair-shtend-niss*

Mr.	Herr/-en	*hair*
Mrs.	Frau	*fr'ow*
model	(das) Modell/-e	*MO-del*
modern	modern, -er, -e, -es	*mo-DAIRN*
moment	(der) Moment/-en	*mo-MENT*
Monday	(der) Montag/-e	*MOHN-tahk*
money	(das) Geld	*ghelt*
monkey	(der) Affe/-n	*AHF-eh*
month	(der) Monat/-e	*MO-naht*
monument	(das) Denkmal/-mäler	*DENK-mahl*
moon	(der) Mond	*mohnt*
more	mehr	*mair*
morning	(der) Morgen/—	*MORE-ghen*
mostly	meistens	*MY-stens*
mother	(die) Mutter/Mütter	*MOOT-ter*
mother-in-law	(die) Schwiegermutter/-mütter	*SHVEE-gher-moot-ter*
motor	(der) Motor/-en	*MO-tohr*
motorcycle	(das) Motorrad/-räder	*MO-tohr-raht*

mountain	(der) Berg/-e	*bairk*
mouth	(der) Mund/ Münder	*moont*
mouse	(die) Maus/ Mäuse	*m'owss*
movies	(das) Kino/-s	*KEE-no*
much	viel	*feel*
museum	(das) Muse- um/Museen	*moo-ZAY-oom*
music	(die) Musik	*moo-ZEEK*
musician	(der) Musi- ker/—	*MOO-zee-ker*
must	müssen	*MÜSS'en*
I must go.	Ich muß gehen.	*ikh mooss GAY'en.*
mustache	(der) Schnurr- bart/-bärte	*SHNOOR-bart*
mustard	(der) Senf	*zenf*
my	mein (m), meine (f), mein (n); meine (pl)	*mine, MINE-eh*

N

name	(der) Name/-n	*NA-meh*
napkin	(die) Ser- viette/-n	*zairv-YET-eh*
narrow	eng, -er, -e, -es,	*ehng*

navy	(die) Ma-rine/-n	ma-REE-neh
near	nahe, -er, -e, -es,	NA-eh
necessary	notwendig, -er, -e, -es	NOHT-ven-dikh
neck	(der) Nack-en/—	NAHK-en
necktie	(die) Kra-watte/-n	kra-VAHT-eh
(to) need	brauchen	BROW-khen
neighborhood	(die) Nachbar-schaft/-en	NAHKH-bar-shahft
nephew	(der) Neffe/-n	NEF-eh
nervous	nervös, -er, -e, -es,	nair-VERSS
net profit	(der) Rein-gewinn/-e	RINE-ghe-vin
net (weight)	netto	NET-toh
never	niemals	NEE-mahls
Never mind!	Das macht nichts!	dahss makht nikhts!
new	neu, -er, -e, -es,	noy
news	(die) Nach-richt/-en	NAHKH-rikht
newspaper	(die) Zeitung/-en	TS'I-toong
next	nächst, -er, -e, -es,	naixt

nice	nett, -er, -e, -es,	*net*
night	(die) Nacht/ Nächte	*nahkht*
nightclub	(das) Nacht- lokal/-en	*NAHKT-lo-kahl*
nightgown	(das) Nacht- hemd/-e	*NAHKHT-hemt*
nine	neun	*noyn*
nineteen	neunzehn	*NOYN-ts'ayn*
ninety	neunzig	*NOYN-ts'ikh*
no	nein	*nine*
no (not a)	kein (m), keine (f), kein (n); keine (pl)	*kine, KY-neh*
nobody	niemand	*NEE-mahnt*
noise	(der) Lärm	*lairm*
none	keine	*KY-neh*
noon	(der) Mittag/-e	*MIT-tahk*
north	(der) Norden	*NOR-den*
nose	(die) Nase/-n	*NA-zeh*
not	nicht	*nikht*
not any	kein, keine, kein	*kine, KY-neh*
not yet	noch nicht	*nohkh nikht*
nothing	nichts	*nikhts*
nothing at all	garnichts	*GAR-nikhts*

November	(der) November	*no-VEM-ber*
now	jetzt	*yetst*
nowhere	nirgends	*NEER-ghents*
number	(die) Num-mer/–	*NOOM-er*

O

occasionally	dann und wann	*dahn oont vahn*
occupied	besetzt, -er, -e, -es	*beh-ZETST*
ocean	(der) Ozean/-e	*OH-ts'eh-ahn*
October	(der) Oktober	*ok-TOH-ber*
of	von	*fohn*
of the	des (m, n), der (f); der (pl)	*dess* *dair* *dair*
off	ab	*ahp*
(to) offer	*anbieten* (SP)	*AHN-beet'en*
office	(das) Büro/-s	*BÜ-ro*
officer	(der) Offizier/-e	*off-fee-TS'EER*
official	(der) Beam-te/-n	*beh-AHM-teh*
often	oft	*ohft*
oil	(das) Öl	*erl*
O.K.	alles in Ordnung	*AH-less in ORD-noong*

old	alt, -er, -e, -es,	*ahlt*
on	auf	*ow'f*
on the	auf dem (m, n)	*owf daim*
	auf der (f)	*owf dair*
	auf den (pl)	*owf dain*
on time	pünktlich, -er, -e, -es	*PÜNKT-likh*
once	einst	*ine'st*
At once!	Sofort!	*zo-FORT!*
one	ein, -er, -e,	*ine*
only	nur	*noor*
onto the	auf den (m)	*owf dain*
	auf die (f)	*owf dee*
	auf das *or* aufs (n)	*owf dahss, owfs*
	auf die (pl)	*owf dee*
open	offen, -er, -e, -es	*OHF'en*
(to) open	öffnen	*ERF-nen*
opera	(die) Oper/-n	*OH-per*
opinion	(die) Mei-nung/-en	*MINE-oong*
opportunity	(die) Gelegen-heit/-en	*ghe-LAIG-en-hite*
opposite	gegenüber	*ghe-ghe-NÜ-ber*
or	oder	*OH-der*
orange	(die) Apfel-sine/-n	*ahp-fel-ZEE-neh*
orchestra	(das) Orche-ster/—	*or-KEH-ster*

order	(der) Befehl/-e	beh-FAIL
(to) order	bestellen	beh-SHTEL'en
in order to	um . . . zu	oom . . . ts'oo
original	ursprünglich, -er, -e, -es,	OOR-shprüng-likh
other	anderer, andere, anderes	AHN-der-er
ought	sollen	ZOHL'en
You ought to . . .	Sie sollten . . .	zee ZOHLT'en
our	unser (m), unsere (f), unser (n); unsere (pl)	OON-zer OON-ser-eh
outside	draußen	DR'OW-sen
over	über	Ü-ber
(to) owe	schulden	SHOOL-den
(to) own	besitzen	beh-ZITS'en
owner	(der) Besit-zer/—	beh-ZIT-ser
ox	(der) Ochse/-n	ohx

P

package	(das) Paket/-te	pa-KET
paid	bezahlt	beh-TS'AHLT
pain	(der) Schmerz/-en	shmairts

(to) paint	malen	*MAHL'en*
painting	(das) Gemäl-de/—	*ghe-MAYL-deh*
palace	(das) Schloß/ Schlösser	*shlohss*
pants	(die) Hose/-n	*HO-zeh*
paper	(das) Papier/-e	*pa-PEER*
parade	(die) Pa-rade/-n	*pa-RAHD-eh*
Pardon me!	Entschuldigen Sie!	*ent-SHOOL-dig'en zeel*
(to) park	parken	*PARK'en*
park	(der) Park	*park*
parents	(die) Eltern	*EL-tern*
part	(der) Teil/-e	*tile*
partner (busi-ness)	(der) Teil-haber/—	*TILE-hahb-er*
passenger	(der) Fahr-gast/-gäste	*FAR-gahst*
passport	(der) Pass/ Pässe	*pahss*
past	(die) Vergan-genheit	*fair-GAHNG-en-hite*
(to) pay	zahlen	*TS'AHL'en*
peace	(der) Frieden	*FREE-den*
pen	(die) Schreib-feder/—	*SHRIPE-fay-der*
pencil	(der) Blei-stift/-e	*BLY-shtift*

people	(die) Leute	*LOY-teh*
percent	(das) Prozent	*pro-TS'ENT*
perfect	vollkommen, -er, -e, es	*fohl-KOHM'en*
perfume	(das) Parfüm/-e	*par-FÜM*
perhaps	vielleicht	*feel-LY'KHT*
permitted	erlaubt, -er, -e, -es	*air-L'OWPŢ*
person	(die) Person/-en	*per-ZOHN*
photo	(das) Foto/-s	*FO-toh*
piano	(das) Klavier/-e	*klah-VEER*
picture	(das) Bild/-er	*bilt*
piece	(das) Stück/-e	*stŭk*
pier	(der) Pier/-s	*peer*
pill	(die) Pille/-n	*PIL-eh*
pillow	(das) Kissen/—	*KISS'en*
pin	(die) Stecknadel/—	*SHTEK-nahd-el*
pink	rosa	*RO-za*
pipe (smoking)	(die) Pfeife/-n	*P'FY-feh*
place	(der) Platz/Plätze	*plahts*
plan	(der) Plan/Pläne	*plahn*
plane (airplane)	(das) Flugzeug/-e	*FLOOK-ts'oyk*

planet	(der) Planet/ -en	*pla-NEHT*
plant (garden)	(die) Pflanze/ -n	*P'FLAHN-ts'eh*
plant (factory)	(die) Fabrik- anlage/-n	*fa-BRICK-ahn-la- gheh*
plate	(der) Teller/—	*TEL-er*
(to) play	spielen	*SHPEEL'en*
pleasant	angenehm, -er, -e, -es	*AHN-ghe-naim*
Please!	Bitte!	*BIT-teh*
pleasure	(das) Vergnü- gen/—	*fairg-NÜG-en*
pocket	(die) Tasche/-n	*TA-sheh*
poem	(das) Ge- dicht/-e	*ghe-DIKHT*
(to) point out	zeigen	*TS'Y-ghen*
Poland	(das) Polen	*PO-len*
Pole (person)	(der) Pole/-n (die) Polin/ -nen	*PO-leh* *PO-lin*
policeman	(der) Polizist/ -en	*po-leets-ISST*
police station	(die) Polizei- wache	*po-leets-EYE-va-khe*
Polish	polnisch, -er, -e, -es	*POHL-nish*
polite	höflich -er, -e, -es,	*HERF-likh*

poor	arm, -er, -e, -es,	*arm*
pope	(der) Papst/ Päpste	*pahpst*
popular	beliebt, -er,	*beh-LEEPT*
pork	(das) Schweine- fleisch	*SHVY-ne-fly'sh*
Portugal	(das) Portugal	*PORT-oo-gahl*
possible	möglich, -er, -e, -es	*MERG-likh*
postcard	(die) Post- karte/-n	*POHST-kar-teh*
post office	(das) Postamt/ -ämter	*POHST-ahmt*
potato	(die) Kar- toffel/-n	*kar-TOFF-el*
pound (weight)	(das) Pfund/-e	*pfoont*
(to) practice	üben	*Ü-ben*
(to) prefer	vorziehen (SP)	*FOR-ts'ee'en*
pregnant	schwanger, -er, -e, -es	*SHVAHNG-er*
(to) prepare	vorbereiten (SP)	*FOR-beh-rite'en*
present (gift)	(das) Ge- schenk/-e	*ghe-SHENK*
president	(der) Präsi- dent/-en	*preh-zee-DENT*
(to) press (clothes)	bügeln	*BÜG-eln*

pretty	hübsch, -er, -e, -es	*hüpsh*
previously	vorher	*FOR-hair*
price	(der) Preis/-e	*price*
priest	(der) Priester/—	*PREE-ster*
prince	(der) Prinz/-e	*prints*
princess	(die) Prinzessin/-nen	*prints-ESS-in*
prison	(das) Gefängnis/-se	*ghe-FENG-niss*
private	privat, -er, -e, -es,	*pree-VAHT*
probable	wahrscheinlich, -er, -e, -es	*VAR-shine-likh*
problem	(das) Problem/-e	*pro-BLAYM*
production	(die) Produktion	*pro-dook-TS'YOHN*
profession	(der) Beruf/-e	*beh-ROOF*
profits	(der) Profit	*pro-FEET*
professor	(der) Professor/-en	*pro-FESS-or*
program	(das) Programm/-e	*pro-GRAHM*
(to) promise	versprechen	*fair-SHPREKH'en*
(to) pronounce	*aus*sprechen (SP)	*OWSS-shprekh'en*
propaganda	(die) Propaganda	*pro-pa-GAHN-da*

property	(das) Eigentum	*EYE-ghen-toom*
Protestant	(der). Prote-stant/-en	*pro-test-AHNT.*
public	öffentlich, -er, -e, -es	*ERF-ent-likh*
publicity	(die) Öffent-lichkeit	*ERF-ent-likh-kite*
publisher	(der) Ver-leger/—	*fair-LAIG-er*
(to) pull	ziehen	*TS'EE'en*
(to) purchase	kaufen	*KOWF'en*
purple	purpurfarben	*poor-POOR-far-ben*
purse	(der) Geld-beutel/—	*GHELT-boy-tel*
(to) push	schieben	*SHEEB'en*
(to) put down	*hin*legen (SP)	*HIN-laig'en*
(to) put on	*an*legen (SP)	*AHN-laig'en*

Q

quality	(die) Quali-tät/-en	*kva-lee-TAIT*
queen	(die) Köni-gin/-nen	*KERN-ig-in*
question	(die) Frage/-n	*FRA-gheh*
quick	schnell, -er, -e, -es,	*shnel*
quiet	still, -er, -e, -es,	*shtil*
quite	ganz	*gahnts*

R

Rabbi	(der) Rabbi-ner/–	*ra-BIN-er*
rabbit	(das) Kanin-chen/–	*kahn-EEN-khen*
race (contest)	(das) Wettren-nen/–	*VET-ren'en*
radio	(das) Radio/-s	*RA-dee-o*
railroad	(die) Eisen-bahn/-en	*EYE-zen-bahn*
(to) rain	regnen	*RAYG'nen*
It's raining!	Es regnet!	*ess RAYG-net!*
raincoat	(der) Regen-mantel/-mäntel	*RAY-ghen-mahn-tel*
rarely	selten	*ZEL-ten*
rate (of exchange)	(der) Kurs	*koorss*
razor	(der) Rasierap-parat/-e	*ra-ZEER-ahp-par-aht*
(to) read	lesen	*LAYZ'en*
ready (finished)	fertig, -er, -e, -es	*FAIR-tikh*
real	wirklich, -er, -e, -es	*VEER-klikh*
receipt	(die) Quit-tung/-en	*KVIT-toong*
(to) receive	erhalten	*air-HAHLT'en*

recent	kürzlich, -er, -e, -es,	*KÜRTS-likh*
(to) recognize	erkennen	*air-KEN'en*
(to) recommend	empfehlen	*emp-FAIL'en*
red	rot, -er, -e, -es,	*roht*
refrigerator	(der) Kühl-schrank/-schränke	*KÜL-shrahnk*
(to) refuse	*ab*schlagen (SP)	*AHP-shlag'en*
(My) regards to . . .	Meine Grüße an . . .	*MINE-eh GRÜ-seh ahn . . .*
regular	regelrecht, -er, -e, -es,	*RAY-ghel-rekht*
religion	(die) Reli-gion/-en	*reh-lee-G'YOHN*
(to) remain	bleiben	*BLY-ben*
(to) remember	sich erinnern	*zikh eh-RIN-ern*
(to) rent	mieten	*MEET'en*
(to) repair	reparieren	*reh-par-EER'en*
(to) repeat	wiederholen	*vee-der-HO-len*
report	(der) Be-richt/-e	*beh-RIKHT*
(to) represent	repräsentieren	*reh-pray-ZEN-TEER'en*
representative	(der) Vertre-ter/-	*fair-TRAY-er*
responsible	verantwort-lich, -er, -e, -es	*fair-AHNT-vort-likh*

(the) rest	(das) Übrige	*ÜB-rig-eh*
(to) rest	sich *aus*ruhen (SP)	*zikh OW'SS-roo'en*
restaurant	(das) Restaurant/-s	*res-toh-RAHNG*
(to) return	*zurück*kehren (SP)	*ts'oo-RÜK-kair'en*
revolution	(die) Revolution/-en	*reh-vo-loo-TS'YOHN*
reward	(die) Belohnung/-en	*beh-LO-noong*
rich	reich, -er, -e, -es	*ry'kh*
(to) ride (a horse)	reiten	*RY-ten*
(to) ride (in a vehicle)	fahren (mit)	*FAR'en*
right (not left)	rechts	*rekhts*
right (correct)	richtig, -er, -e, -es	*RIKH-tikh*
Right away!	Sofort!	*zo-FORT!*
ring	(der) Ring/-e	*ring*
riot	(der) Aufruhr/-en	*OWF-roor*
river	(der) Fluß/ Flüsse	*flooss*
road	(der) Weg/-e	*vaik*
roof	(das) Dach/ Dächer	*dakh*

room	(das) Zim-mer/–	*TS'IM-er*
room service	(die) Zimmer-bedienung	*TS'IM-er-beh-dee-noong*
round trip	(die) Rund-fahrt/-en	*ROONT-fahrt*
route	(der) Weg/-e	*vek*
rug	(der) Tep-pich/-e	*TEP-ikh*
(to) run	laufen	*L'OW-fen*
Russia	(das) Ruß-land	*ROOSS-lahnt*
Russian	russisch, -er, -e, -es	*ROOSS-ish*
Russian (person)	(der) Russe/-n (die) Rus-sin-nen	*ROOSS-eh ROOSS-in*

S

sad	traurig, -er, -e, -es	*TR'OW-rikh*
safe	sicher, -er, -e, -es	*ZIK-kher*
said	gesagt	*ghe-ZAKT*
sailor	(der) See-mann/ -leute	*(der) ZAY-mahn*
saint	(der, die) Heilige	*HI-lee-ghe*

salad	(der) Salat	*za-LAHT*
salary	(das) Gehalt/ Gehälter	*ghe-HAHLT*
sale	(der) Ver- kauf/Ver- käufe	*fair-KOWF*
same	derselbe, diesel- be, dasselbe	*dair-ZEL-beh, dee- ZEL-beh, dahss- ZEL-beh*
sandwich	(das) belegte Butterbrot	*beh-LAIK-teh boot-er-BROHT*
Saturday	(der) Sams- tag/-e	*ZAHMSS-tahk*
(to) say	sagen	*ZAHG'en*
school	(die) Schule/-n	*SHOOL-eh*
scissors	(die) Schere/-n	*SHAIR-eh*
Scotch	schottisch, -er, -e, -es	*SHOHT-tish*
Scotchman	(der) Schot- te/-n	*SHOHT-teh*
Scotch woman	(die) Schottin/ -nen	*SHOHT-tin*
Scotland	Schottland	*SHOHT-lahnt*
sea	(das) Meer/-e	*mair*
season	(die) Jahres- zeit/-en	*YAR-ess-ts'ite*
secretary	(der) Sekretär/ -e	*saik-re-TAIR*
	(die) Sekre- tärin/-nen	*saik-re-TAIR-in*

(to) see	sehen	*ZAY'en*
seen	gesehen	*ghe-ZAY'en*
seldom	selten	*ZEL-ten*
(to) sell	verkaufen	*fair-KOW-fen*
(to) send	schicken	*SHIK'en*
(to) send for	holen lassen	*HO-len LAHSS'en*
separate	verschieden, -er, -e, -es	*fair-SHEE-den*
September	(der) September	*sep-TEM-ber*
serious	ernst, -er, -e, -es	*airnst*
service	(der) Dienst/-e	*deenst*
service (hotel, restaurant)	(die) Bedienung/-en	*beh-DEEN-oong*
seven	sieben	*ZEE-ben*
seventeen	siebzehn	*ZEEP-ts'ayn*
seventy	siebzig	*ZEEP-ts'ikh*
several	mehrere	*MAIR-er-eh*
shares (stock)	(die) Aktien	*AHK-ts'ee-en*
shark	(der) Haifisch/-e	*HI-fish*
sharp	scharf, -er, -e, -es	*sharf*
she	sie	*zee*
ship	(das) Schiff/-e	*shif*
shirt	(das) Hemd/-en	*hemt*

shoe	(der) Schuh/-e	*shoo*
shop	(der) Laden/ Läden	*LA-den*
short	kurz, -er, -e, -es	*koorts*
should (ought to)		
I (he, she, it) should	ich (er, sie, es) sollte	*ikh (air, zee, ess) ZOHL-teh*
you (we, they) should	Sie (wir, sie) sollten	*zee (veer, zee) ZOHL-ten*
shoulder	(die) Schulter/-n	*SHOOL-ter*
show	(die) Schau	*sh'ow*
(to) show	zeigen	*TS'I-ghen*
Show me!	Zeigen Sie mir!	*TS'I-ghen zee meer!*
shower	(das) Brause- bad/-bäder	*BROW-zeh-baht*
(to) shut	schliessen	*SHLEE-sen*
sick	krank, -er, -e, -es	*krahnk*
(to) sign	unterschreiben	*oont-er-SHRY-ben*
simple	einfach, -er, -e, -es	*INE-fakh*
sincere	aufrichtig, -er, -e, -es	*OWF-rikh-tikh*
(to) sing	singen	*ZING'en*
singer	(der) Sänger/—	*ZENG-er*
sir	mein Herr	*mine hair*

sister	(die) Schwester/-n	SHVESS-ter
sister-in-law	(die) Schwägerin/-nen	SHVAIG-er-in
(to) sit	sitzen	ZITZ'en
Sit down!	Setzen Sie sich!	ZETZ'en zee zikh!
six	sechs	zex
sixteen	sechzehn	ZEKH-ts'ayn
sixty	sechzig	ZEKH-ts'ikh
size	(die) Größe/-n	GRER-seh
skin	(die) Haut/ Häute	howt
skirt	(der) Rock/ Röcke	rohk
sky	(der) Himmel	HIM-el
(to) sleep	schlafen	SHLA-fen
slow	langsam, -er, -e, -es	LAHNG-zahm
small	klein, -er, -e, -es	kline
(to) smoke	rauchen	ROW-khen
snow	(der) Schnee	shnay
so	so	zo
soap	(die) Seife/-n	ZY-fe
soft	weich, -er, -e, -es	vy'kh
soldier	(der) Soldat/ -en	zol-DAHT

some (a little)	etwas	*ET-vahss*
some (several)	einige	*INE-ig-eh*
somebody	jemand	*YEH-mahnt*
something	etwas	*ET-vahss*
sometimes	manchmal	*MAHNKH-mahl*
somewhere	irgendwo	*EER-ghent-vo*
son	(der) Sohn/ Söhne	*zohn*
song	(das) Lied/-er	*leet*
soon	bald	*bahlt*
(I am) sorry.	Es tut mir leid.	*ess toot meer lite.*
soup	(die) Suppe/-n	*ZOOP-eh*
south	(der) Süden	*ZÜD-en*
South America	Süd-Amerika	*ZÜD-ah-mair-ik-ah*
South American	südamerika- nisch, -er, -e, -es	*züd-ah-mair- ik-AH-nish*
South American (person)	(der) Südameri- kaner	*ZÜD-ah-mair- ik-ahn-er*
	(die) Südameri- kanerin	*ZÜD-ah-mair- ik-ahn-er-in*
Spain	(das) Spanien	*SHPAHN-yen*
Spaniard	(der) Spanier/— (die) Spa- nierin/-nen	*SHPAHN-ee-yer* *SHPAHN-ee-yer-in*

Spanish	spanisch, -er, -e, es	*SHPAHN-ish*
(to) speak	sprechen	*SHPREKH'en*
special	besonder, -er, -e, es	*beh-ZOHN-der*
(to) spend (money)	*aus*geben (SP)	*OWSS-gay-ben*
(to) spend (time)	verbringen	*fair-BRING'en*
spoon	(der) Löffel/—	*LERF-el*
sport	(der) Sport/-s	*shport*
spring	(der) Frühling/-e	*FRÜ-ling*
stamp (postage)	(die) Brief-marke/-n	*BREEF-mark-eh*
star	(der) Stern/-e	*shtairn*
(to) start	*an*fangen (SP)	*AHN-fahng'en*
station (railroad)	(der) Bahn-hof/-höfe	*BAHN-hohf*
(to) stay	bleiben	*BLY-ben*
steel	(der) Stahl	*shtahl*
still (quiet, not moving)	ruhig, -er, -e, -es	*ROO-ikh*
still (time)	noch immer	*nokh IM-er*
stockmarket	(die) Börse/-n	*BER-zeh*
stone	(der) Stein/-e	*shtine*
Stop!	Halt!	*hahlt!*
(to) stop (something)	*Auf*hören! (SP)	*OWF-her'en*

store	(der) Laden/ Läden	*LA-den*
storm	(der) Sturm/ Stürme	*shtoorm*
story	(die) Geschichte/ -n	*ghe-SHIKH-teh*
strange (odd)	sonderbar, -er, -e, -es	*ZOHN-der-bar*
street	(die) Straße/-n	*SHTRAHSS-eh*
strong	stark, -er, -e, -es	*shtark*
student	(der) Student/-en	*shtoo-DENT*
(to) study	studieren	*shtoo-DEER'en*
subway	(die) Untergrundbahn/-en	*OONT-er-groont-bahn*
sudden	plötzlich, -er, -e, -es	*PLERTZ-likh*
sugar	(der) Zucker	*TS'OOK-er*
suit (clothes)	(der) Anzug/Anzüge	*AHN-ts'ook*
suitcase	(der) Handkoffer	*HAHNT-koff-er*
summer	(der) Sommer/–	*ZOHM-er*
sun	(die) Sonne	*ZO-ne*

Sunday	(der) Sonntag/-e	*ZOHN-tahk*
sure	sicher, -er, -e, -es	*ZIKH-er*
surprise	(die) Überraschung	*û-ber-RAHSH-oong*
sweet	süß, -er, -e, -es	*züss*
(to) swim	schwimmen	*SHVIM'en*
swimming pool	(das) Schwimmbassin/-s	*SHVIM-ba-sin*
Swiss	schweizerisch, -er, -e, -es	*SHVY-ts'er-ish*
Swiss (person)	(der) Schweizer/—	*SHVY-ts'er*
	(die) Schweizerin/-nen	*SHVY-ts'-er-in*
Switzerland	(die) Schweiz	*shvy'ts*

T

table	(der) Tisch/-e	*tish*
tailor	(der) Schneider/—	*SHNY-der*
(to) take	nehmen	*NAYM'en*
(to) take a walk	spazieren gehen	*shpa-TS'EER'en GAY'en*
(to) talk	reden	*RAYD'en*
tall	groß, -er, -e, -es	*grohss*

tape	(das) Band/Bänd-er	*bahnt*
tape recorder	(das) Ton-bandgerät	*TOHN-bahnt-ghe-rait*
tax	(die) Steuer/-n	*SHTOY-er*
taxi	(das) Taxi/-s	*TAHK-see*
tea	(der) Tee	*tay*
(to) teach	lehren	*LAIR'en*
teacher	(der) Lehrer/— (die) Leh-rerin/-nen	*LAIR-er* *LAIR-er-in*
team	(die) Mann-schaft/-en	*MAHN-shahft*
telegram	(das) Tele-gramm	*teh-leh-GRAHM*
telephone	(das) Telephon/-e	*teh-leh-FOHN*
television	(das) Fernsehen	*FAIRN-zay'en*
(to) tell	erzählen	*air-TS'AIL'en*
Tell him (her) ...	Erzähle ihm (ihr) ...	*air-TS'AIL-eh eem (eer)*
temperature	(die) Tem-peratur/-en	*tem-per-ah-TOOR*
ten	zehn	*ts'ayn*
terrible	furchtbar, -er, -e, -es	*FOORKHT-bar*
than	als	*ahls*

(to) thank	danken	*DAHNK'en*
Thank you!	Danke!	*DAHN-keh*
that (one)	das	*dahss*
that	daß	*dahss*
the	der (m), die (f), das (n); die (pl)	*dair, dee, dahss, dee*
theater	(das) Theater/—	*teh-AH-ter*
their	ihr (m), ihre (f), ihr (n); ihre (pl)	*eer, eer-eh, eer, eer-eh*
them	sie	*zee*
(to) them	ihnen	*EEN-en*
then	dann	*dahn*
there	dort	*dort*
there is, there are	es gibt	*ess ghipt*
therefore	deswegen	*DESS-vayg-en*
these	diese	*DEE-ze*
they	sie	*zee*
thin	dünn,-er, -es,-e	*dûn*
thing	(die) Sache/-n	*ZA-kheh*
(to) think	denken	*DEHNK'en*
third	dritt, -er, -e, -es	*drit*
thirsty	durstig, -er, -e, -es	*DOOR-stikh*

thirteen	dreizehn	*DRY-ts'ayn*
thirty	dreißig	*DRY-sikh*
this	dies, -er, -e, -es	*dees*
those	jene	*YEH-neh*
thousand	(das) Tausend/-e	*T'OW-zent*
thread	(der) Faden/Fäden	*FA-den*
three	drei	*dry*
throat	(die) Gurgel/-n	*GOOR-ghel*
through	durch	*doorkh*
Thursday	(der) Donnerstag/-e	*DOHN-ers-tahk*
ticket (train)	(die) Fahrkarte/-n	*FAR-kar-te*
tie	(die) Krawatte/-n	*kra-VA-te*
tiger	(der) Tiger/—	*TEE-gher*
time	(die) Zeit/-en	*ts'ite*
tip	(das) Trinkgeld/-er	*TRINK-ghelt*
tire (auto)	(der) Reifen/—	*RY-fen*
tired	müde, müder, müde, müdes	*MÜD-eh*
to (direction)	nach	*nahkh*
to (in order to)	um . . . zu	*oom . . . ts'oo*

to the	dem (m, n)	*dem*
(indirect	der (f)	*dair*
object)	den (pl)	*den*
to the (place)	zu dem *or* zum (m, n)	*ts'oo dem, ts'oom*
	zu der *or* zur (f)	*ts'oo dair, ts'oor*
	zu den (pl)	*ts'oo den*
tobacco	(der) Tabak	*TA-bahk*
today	heute	*HOY-teh*
together	zusammen	*ts'oo-ZA-men*
tomorrow	morgen	*MOHR-gen*
tomorrow morning	morgen früh	*MOHR-gen frü*
tomorrow night	morgen abend	*MOHR-gen AHB-ent*
tongue	(die) Zunge/-n	*TS'OONG-eh*
tonight	heute abend	*HOY-teh AH-bent*
too (also)	auch	*owkh*
too (excessive)	allzu	*AHL-ts'oo*
tooth	(der) Zahn/Zähne	*ts'ahn*
toothbrush	(die) Zahn-bürste/-n	*TS'AHN-bür-ste*
toothpaste	(die) Zahnpaste	*TS'AHN-pa-sta*
tour	(die) Tour/-en	*toor*
towel	(das) Hand-tuch/-tücher	*HAHNT-tookh*

tower	(der) Turm/ Türme	*toorm*
town	(die) Stadt/ Städte	*shtaht*
toy	(das) Spielzeug/-e	*SHPEEL-ts'oyk*
trade fair	(die) Handels- messe/-n	*HAHN-delss-mess-eh*
traffic	(der) Verkehr	*fair-KAIR*
train	(der) Zug/Züge	*ts'ook*
translation	(die) Über- setzung/-en	*ŭ-ber-ZETS-oong*
(to) travel	reisen	*RY-zen*
travel agency	(das) Reisebüro/-s	*RY-ze-bŭ-ro*
traveler	(der) Reisende/-n	*RY-zen-deh*
	(die) Reisende/-n	*RY-zen-deh*
treasurer	(der) Zahl- meister/—	*TS'AHL-my-ster*
tree	(der) Baum/ Bäume	*b'owm*
trip	(die) Reise/-n	*RY-zeh*
trouble (care)	(die) Sorge/-n	*ZORG-eh*
truck	(der) Lastwagen/—	*LAHST-va-ghen*
true	wahr, -er, -e, -es	*var*

(to) try (attempt)	versuchen	*fair-ZOOKH'en*
(to) try (for quality)	probieren	*pro-BEER'en*
Tuesday	(der) Dienstag/-e	*DEENSS-tahk*
Turk	(der) Türke/-n (die) Türkin/ -nen	*TÜR-keh* *TÜR-kin*
Turkey	(die) Türkei	*tŭr-KYE*
Turkish	türkisch, -er, -e, -es	*TÜR-kish*
(to make a) turn	*ab*biegen (SP)	*AHB-beeg'n*
(to) turn off	*ab*stellen (SP)	*AHP-shteľen*
(to) turn on	*an*stellen (SP)	*AHN-shteľen*
twelve	zwölf	*ts'verlf*
twenty	zwanzig	*TS'VAHN-ts'ikh*
two	zwei	*ts'vye*
typewriter	(die) Schreib- maschine/-n	*SHRIPE-ma-shee-neh*

U

ugly	häßlich, -er, -e, -es	*HESS-likh*
umbrella	(der) Regen- schirm/-e	*RAY-ghen-sheerm*
uncle	(der) Onkel/	*OHN-kel*

under	unter	*OON-ter*
(to) understand	verstehen	*fair-SHTAY'en*
Do you understand?	Verstehen Sie?	*fair-SHTAY'en zee?*
I don't understand.	Ich verstehe nicht.	*ikh fair-SHTAY-eh nikht.*
underwear	(die) Unter- kleider (pl)	*OON-ter-kly-der*
unfortunately	leider	*LYE-der*
uniform	(die) Uniform/-en	*oo-nee-FORM*
United States	(die) Vereinig- ten Staaten	*fair-INE-ig-ten SHTAHT-en*
United Nations	(die) Vereinten Nationen	*fair-INE-ten nah-TS'YO-nen*
university	(die) Univer- sität/-en	*oo-nee-vair- zee-TAYT*
until	bis	*biss*
up	hinauf	*hin-OWF*
urgent	dringend, -er, -e, -es	*DRING-ent*
us, to us	uns	*oonss*
(to) use	gebrauchen	*ghe-BROW-khen*
used to (in the habit of . . .)	angewöhnt, -er, -e, -es	*AHN-ghe-vernt*
useful	nützlich, -er, -e, -es	*NÜTS-likh*
usual	gewöhnlich, -er, -e, -es	*ghe-VERN-likh*

V

vacant	unbesetzt, -er, -e, -es	*OON-beh-zetst*
vacation	(der) Urlaub	*OOR-l'owp*
vaccination	(die) Schutz- impfung/-en	*SHOOTZ-imp-foong*
valley	(das) Tal/ Täler	*tahl*
value	wert	*vairt*
various	verschieden, -er, -e, -es	*fair-SHEED-en*
very	sehr	*zair*
very well	sehr gut	*zair goot*
view	(die) Aussicht/-en	*OWSS-sikht*
village	(das) Dorf/Dörfer	*dorf*
(to) visit	besuchen	*beh-ZOOKH'en*
violin	(die) Geige/-n	*GHY-gheh*
voice	(die) Stimme/-n	*SHTIM-eh*
voyage	(die) Reise/-n	*RY-zeh*

W

(to) wait	warten	*VAR-ten*
waiter	(der) Kellner/—	*KELL-ner*

waitress	(die) Kellner-in/-nen	*KELL-ner-in*
(to) walk	gehen	*GAY'en*
wall	(die) Wand/Wände	*vahnt*
wallet	(die) Geld-tasche/-n	*GHELT-ta-sheh*
(to) want	wollen	*VOHL'en*
I want	ich will	*vill*
he (she) wants	er (sie) will	*vill*
you (we, they) want	Sie (wir, sie) wollen	*VOHL'en*
Do you want . . . ?	Wollen Sie . . . ?	*VOHL'en zee . . . ?*
war	(der) Krieg/-e	*kreek*
warm	warm, -er, -e, -es	*varm*
(I, he, she, it) was	(ich, er, sie, es) war	*var*
(to) wash	waschen	*VAHSH'en*
watch	(die) Uhr/-en	*oor*
(to) watch	anschauen (SP)	*AHN-sh'ow'en*
Watch out!	Aufpassen!	*OWF-pahss'en*
water	(das) Wasser	*VAHSS-er*
way	(der) Weg/-e	*vehk*
we	wir	*veer*

weak	schwach, -er, -e, -es,	shvahkh
(to) wear	tragen	TRA-ghen
weather	(das) Wetter	VET-er
wedding	(die) Hoch-zeit/-en	HOKH-ts'ite
Wednesday	(der) Mitt-woch/-e	MIT-vokhk
week	(die) Woche/-n	VO-khe
weekend	(das) Wochen-ende/-n	VO-khen-end-eh
Welcome!	Willkommen!	veel-KOHM'en!
You are welcome.	Bitte schön!	BIT-teh shern!
well	gut	goot
went		
I went	ich bin ge-gangen	geh-GAHNG-en
he (she, it) went	er (sie, es) ist gegangen	air (zee, ess) isst
you (we, they) went	Sie (wir, sie) sind gegan-gen	zee (veer, zee) zint
(you, we, they) were	(Sie, wir, sie) waren	VAR'en
west	(der) Westen	VEST-en
what	was	vahss
What's the matter?	Was ist los?	vahss isst lohss?

What time is it?	Wie spät ist es?	*vee shpayt isst ess?*
when?	wann?	*vahn?*
when (while)	als	*ahlss*
where?	wo?	*vo?*
Where to?	Wohin?	*vo-HIN?*
whether	ob	*ohp*
which?	der, die, das,	*dair, dee, dahss*
while	während	*VAIR-ent*
white	welcher, welche, welches?	*VEL-kher?*
who?	wer?	*vair?*
who	der, die, das,	*dair, dee, dahss*
whole	ganz, -er, -e, -es	*gahnts*
whom?	wen?	*vain?*
whose?	wessen?	*VESS-en?*
why?	warum?	*va-ROOM?*
wide	breit, -er, -e, -es	*brite*
widow	(die) Witwe/-n	*VIT-veh*
widower	(der) Witwer/—	*VIT- ver*
wife	(die) Frau/-en	*fr'ow*
wild	wild, -er, -e, es,	*vilt*
will		
I will	ich werde	*ikh VAIR-deh*

he (she, it) will	er, (sie, es) wird	*air (zee, ess) veert*
you (we, they) will	Sie, (wir, sie) werden	*zee (veer, zee) VAIR-den*
(to) win	gewinnen	*ghe-VINN'en*
wind	(der) Wind/-e	*vint*
window	(das) Fenster/—	*FEN-ster*
wine	(der) Wein/-e	*vine*
winter	(der) Winter/—	*VIN-ter*
wish	(der) Wunsch/- Wünsche	*voonsh*
(to) wish	wünschen	*VÜN-shen*
without	ohne	*OH-ne*
with the	mit dem (m, n) mit der (f) mit den (pl)	*mit daim mit dair mit dain*
wolf	(der) Wolf/ Wölfe	*vohlf*
woman	(die) Frau/-en	*fr'ow*
wonderful	wunderbar, -er, -e, -es	*VOON-der-bar*

won't
Use nicht with the forms of werden. (See "will.")

wood	(der) Wald/ Wälder	*vahlt*
wool	(die) Wolle	*VO-le*
word	(das) Wort/ Wörter	*vort*

work	(die) Arbeit/-en	*AR-bite*
(to) work	arbeiten	*AR-bite'en*
world	(die) Welt/-en	*velt*
worse	schlechter, -er, -e, -es	*SHLEKHT-er*

would

I (he, she, it) would	ich (er, sie, es) würde	*ikh (air, zee, ess) VÜR-deh*
you (we, they) would	Sie (wir, sie) würden	*zee (veer, zee) VÜR-den*
Would you ...?	Würden Sie ... ?	*VÜR-den zee ... ?*
I would like ...	Ich möchte ...	*ikh MERKH-teh ...*
Would you like ...?	Möchten Sie ... ?	*MERKH-ten zee ... ?*
(to) write	schreiben	*SHRY-ben*
Write it!	Schreiben Sie es!	*SHRY-ben zee ess!*
writer	(der) Schrift-steller/—	*SHRIFT-shtel-er*
	(die) Schrift-stellerin/-nen	*SHRIFT-shtel-er-in*
wrong	falsch, -er, -e, -es	*fahlsh*

Y

| year | (das) Jahr/-e | *yar* |
| yellow | gelb, -er, -e, -es | *ghelp* |

yes	ja	*ya*
yesterday	gestern	*GHEH-stern*
yet	jedoch	*yeh-DOHKH*
you	Sie (polite, sing or pl)	*zee*
young	jung, -er, -e, -es	*yoong*
your	Ihr (m), Ihre (f) Ihr (n); Ihre (pl)	*eer, EER-eh*

Z

| zipper | (der) Reißver- schluß/ -schlüsse | *RICE-fair-shlooss* |
| zoo | (der) Zoó/-s | *ts'o* |

Point to the Answer

For speedy reference and, when in doubt, to get a clear answer to a question you have just asked, show the following phrase to the person you are addressing and let *him* point to the answer.

Zum leichteren Verständnis Ihrer Antwort auf meine Frage, suchen Sie sich die passende Antwort aus den folgenden Beispielen heraus und deuten Sie bitte auf die zutreffende Antwort.

| Ja. | Nein. | Vielleicht. |
| Yes. | No. | Perhaps. |

| Bestimmt. | In Ordnung. | Entschuldigung. |
| Certainly. | All right. | Excuse me. |

| Ich verstehe. | Ich verstehe nicht. |
| I understand. | I don't understand. |

| Was möchten Sie? | Ich weiß. | Ich weiß nicht. |
| What do you want? | I know. | I don't know. |

| Offen. | Geschlossen. | Zu viel. | Nicht genug. |
| Open. | Closed. | Too much. | Not enough. |

| Kein Zugang. | Es ist verboten. |
| No admittance. | It is forbidden. |

| Einverstanden. | Sehr gut. | Es ist nicht gut. |
| It is agreed. | Very good. | It isn't good. |

| Es ist in der Nähe. | Zu weit. | Sehr weit. |
| It's near. | Too far. | Very far. |

| Links abbiegen! | Rechts abbiegen! |
| Turn left! | Turn right! |

| Immer geradeaus! | Kommen Sie mit mir! |
| Go straight ahead! | Come with me! |

| Warten Sie auf mich. | Ich muß gehen. |
| Wait for me. | I must go. |

| Kommen Sie später zurück. | Ich bin gleich wieder da. |
| Come back later. | I'll be right back. |

| Mein Name ist ——. | Ihr Name? |
| My name is ——. | Your name? |

| Telefonnummer? | Adresse? |
| Telephone number? | Address? |